The Bullwhacker

William Francis Hooker, the author, as he appears today.

THE
BULLWHACKER
Adventures of a Frontier Freighter

By William Francis Hooker

Introduction by David Dary

Edited by Howard R. Driggs

Illustrated with drawings by
Herman Palmer

University of Nebraska Press
Lincoln and London

Introduction copyright © 1988 by the University of Nebraska Press
Manufactured in the United States of America

First Bison Book printing: 1988

Most recent printing indicated by the first digit below:
1   2   3   4   5   6   7   8   9   10

Library of Congress Cataloging in Publication Data
Hooker, William Francis, 1856–1938.
    The bullwhacker: adventures of a frontier freighter / by
William Francis Hooker; introduction by David Dary; edited
by Howard R. Driggs; illustrated with drawings by Herman
Palmer.
    p.   cm.
    Reprint. Originally published: Yonkers-on-Hudson: World
Bk. Co., 1924 (pioneer life series).
    "Bison book."
ISBN 0-8032-7238-3 (pbk.)
    1. Hooker, William Francis, 1856–1938. 2. Cowboys—
Wyoming—Biography. 3. Wyoming—History. 4. Frontier
and pioneer life—Wyoming. I. Driggs, Howard R. (Howard
Roscoe), 1873–1963. II. Title.
F761.H74 1988
978.7′02′0924—dc19   CIP 87-27969
[B]

Originally published in 1924 by the World Book Company
in its Pioneer Life Series.

INTRODUCTION BY DAVID DARY

Some years ago while researching the lives of wagon freighters, traders, and other entrepreneurs in the nineteenth-century American West, I came across William Francis Hooker's book *The Bullwhacker* in the special collections of a university library. The book was first published in 1924 and reprinted in 1934. It was a couple of months before a book-dealer friend specializing in books about the Old West could locate a copy of the first edition for my library. It cost thirty dollars, an indication of its scarcity, but it was worth the price since it contains the author's recollections as a bullwhacker.

Bullwhacker accounts are uncommon, expecially those as personal as Hooker's. His first-person style captures the flavor and feel of his experiences on the frontier. The fact that Hooker had become a good writer by the time he recorded his recollections strengthens their value as a fine example of Western Americana.

William Francis Hooker was born at 6:30 a.m. on May 17, 1856, at Fond du Lac, Wisconsin, at the southern end of Lake Winnebago. Immediately after he was born his father, a foundry foreman, raced to the plant to head off the day shift of iron molders. He led the workers back to his home only to find flames shooting through the roof. The men rushed inside and rescued Mrs. Hooker and the baby and took them in a skiff across the river to stay at a friend's home. Friends later jokingly recalled that young Bill Hooker's first journey gave him the desire to wander.

In 1867, when Bill was eleven years old, the Hooker family moved to Milwaukee. He did not enjoy school and left, first to sell newspapers and then to work in a series of jobs before ending up in the North Western Railroad yards, where he earned thirty dollars a month.

But then his mother died of tuberculosis, and soon after that his father lost a leg in a foundry accident. Bill Hooker's father turned to politics and served as an assemblyman from Milwaukee's old fifth district. Young Bill, however, feared that he, too, was tubercular. The family doctor supposedly told him to seek a dry climate and "live out-of-doors." He decided to go west.

When Bill Hooker left Milwaukee in late March 1873, he was sixteen years old, weighed 109 pounds, had black hair, black eyes, and a smooth pale face. He carried with him a handbag, a Derringer revolver—he called it a "pop-gun"—and a few knickknacks, plus $85 in cash, a large sum for a boy in those years.

He made his way to Omaha and then west to Cheyenne, where he signed up with a bull-train that was loaded and ready to leave Camp Carlin, at Fort Russell, for Fort Laramie on the North Platte River. Hooker was hired by Nate Williams, a Missourian, who was the wagon boss.

Within a year Bill Hooker was driving lead teams, and by then his once pale and flushed cheeks were bronzed. His once thin arms and skinny legs were toughening and filling out, and the cough he had had a year earlier had disappeared. His weight had increased to 155 pounds.

Not a letter writer, Hooker failed to keep in touch with his father and sister. They became so worried that, through a friend in Wyoming Territory, they had notices posted asking for information about him. The description of the missing boy, however, was that of the 105-pound weakling, not the toughened and filled-out young man now traversing the northern plains. In time young Hooker wrote to his father and told him all was well.

In the fall of 1874 Hooker built a log cabin on La Bonte Creek about twelve miles southeast of present-day Douglas, Wyoming. Cheyenne, the nearest town, was about 250 miles away. During the winter of 1874 and 1875, Hooker lived there with Nicholas Huber, a discharged soldier who was unable to reenlist for the fifth time because he was too old.

Huber apparently taught Hooker much about hunting and surviving in the wilds. They spent most of the winter hunting elk, antelope, black-tailed deer, mountain lions, and other game. During that winter they did not meet another person, but in the spring of 1875 a trapper riding a pony and leading a pack mule carrying traps showed up at the cabin. He told Hooker and Huber that the Sioux had crossed the Platte River and were heading in that direction. the trapper advised them to leave at once. They fled, leaving behind many of their possessions, including skins and robes and a revolver and some traps. Huber headed for Fort Laramie, while Hooker set out on foot for Fort Fetterman. Hooker was then approaching his nineteenth birthday.

Hooker wandered east and soon found work as a cowboy ranching in the Black Hills and then in northern Colorado, a few miles off the Texas Trail, a trail over which Texas Longhorns were driven north into Wyoming and Montana. He returned to bullwhacking for a time, but then a friend suggested they walk east to Omaha from Cheyenne. About half-way across Nebraska, his friend decided to take a job with the railroad, and Hooker continued the journey alone. At Council Bluffs, Iowa, Hooker found a job hauling wood. He then joined a circus in Omaha working as a roustabout while traveling through Iowa to Illinois, where he quit the circus to work as a harvest hand. With money in his pocket, Hooker returned to Wisconsin ready to settle down.

Although some of these experiences are recalled in

detail in the pages that follow, Hooker concentrates on
his early days in the West. His recollections capture the
flavor of the life of a bullwhacker and resident of the
northern plains between 1873 and about 1877. His de-
scriptions of the bullwhacker's life and experiences are
particularly valuable, although Hooker himself spent
only about two years, or half of his time in the West, as a
bullwhacker.

Since Hooker was in his late teens, these were im-
pressionable years. Although *The Bullwhacker* was
written nearly forty years later, during a period of renewed interest in the Old West, it recaptures the fresh-
ness of youth. Some of the stories may have been embel-
lished by the author, who had told them time and time
again before eventually writing them down, but they
make clear that, in hauling supplies to army posts and
Indian reservations far from the railroad, the bullwhacker was engaged in a vital, and dangerous, business.

Bill Hooker does not recount what happened to him
after he left the West and returned to Wisconsin. In
retrospect, his later life is perhaps as interesting as his
early years in the West. Returning to Wisconsin, he
learned the printer's trade and became an itinerant
tramp printer. If he could not find work as a printer, he
found other jobs on the road. At one point he purchased
a team of horses, an old wagon, a couple of barrels of red
mineral paint, and a ladder, and traveled through
southern Wisconsin and northern Illinois painting
barns. Wooden fences were common at the time and he
painted advertisements on them for merchants.

In the early 1880s, Hooker, then in his middle twen-
ties, settled down to work as a printer on a newspaper in
Milwaukee. Through setting type, he learned to write
and added to his somewhat thin formal education. Not
without ambition, he soon became a reporter and then

an editor. During the years that followed he worked as a newspaper editor in Ashland, Wisconsin; Pontiac, Illinois; and Chicago and Milwaukee. At one time or another he worked for every newspaper in Milwaukee.

In 1906 he ran the successful mayoral campaign in Milwaukee for Sherburn M. Becker. He then served as Mayor Becker's secretary and was later appointed his tax commissioner. But Hooker retired from politics after failing to get William Mitchell Lewis elected governor. It was then, in 1910, that he accepted the position of editor of the *Erie Railroad Magazine* in New York City.

While in that position he wrote his recollections of his days in the West. They were first published in a 156-page book titled *The Prairie Schooner* (Chicago: Saul Brothers) in 1918. And in 1923 some of Hooker's recollections were published in New York in a 24-page pamphlet, *Three Old Plainsmen, and Three Other Western Stories; Narrative, Personal Experiences, and Reminiscences.* The pamphlet also included the personal reminiscences of A. H. Baiseley, Ezra Meeker, and Col. George W. Stokes, all early pioneers on the plains.

Soon after the pamphlet appeared, and apparently at the urging of Howard R. Driggs, a professor of English at New York University, Hooker rewrote some of the stories that appeared in *The Prairie Schooner* and added new material, which was published in 1924 in New York City by the World Book Company under the title *The Bullwhacker: Adventures of a Frontier Freighter.* Driggs, who edited the book, wrote an introduction, and Herman Palmer, an eastern illustrator, supplied drawings.

The Bullwhacker is better written than *The Prairie Schooner* and contains more details of Hooker's life in the West. It is not error-free. On page 160 Hooker locates Fort Laramie as being 105 miles east of the site of

Fort Fetterman. In truth, Fort Laramie was southeast of Fort Fetterman.

In 1925, less than a year after *The Bullwhacker* was published, ill health forced Hooker to resign as editor of the railroad magazine. He left New York City and returned to Milwaukee. There he took life easier and wrote a regular column for the *Milwaukee Journal* titled "Glimpses of an Earlier Milwaukee." During these years Hooker's long white hair, mustache, and goatee made him a familiar figure on Milwaukee's streets.

At some point Hooker also wrote a historical novel, *Branded Men and Women.* It was not very successful, and he gave up fiction writing.

In 1932, Bill Hooker, then seventy-seven years, married Mary L. Myers, who was sixty-four years old. She was his third wife. They lived in Milwaukee until 1935, when the couple moved to Bartow, Florida. Although retired, Hooker established an automobile agency, organized a factory to build automobile trailers, wrote a daily column for one or more Florida newspapers, and dabbled in local politics. Early in 1938 his health began to fail. On a Saturday morning, December 24, 1938, William Francis Hooker died. He was eighty-two years old.

In reporting his death on Christmas Day, the *Milwaukee Journal* noted: "He liked best to picture his days in the West, as a mule driver in Wyoming, Indian fighter and poker player. He was in the West in the adventurous decade of the 1870's."

It is good to see his recollections of those colorful days once again available.

AN INTRODUCTION TO THE AUTHOR

It seems a long leap from whacking a seven-yoke team of Texas longhorns out on the old Cheyenne Trail to editing the *Erie Railroad Magazine;* yet that is the leap the author of this rare book has made in the course of his eventful life. No one, meeting for the first time this keen-eyed, gentle-voiced veteran of the newspaper world, would suspect that he had ever played the part of an ox-team freighter — so full of rugged, man-testing adventures. Nor would the stranger get any glimpse into these rich experiences of his earlier life until a confidential relationship was assured through true-blue intentions; for William Francis Hooker has always been reticent when it came to talking about his own unique experiences.

He was induced, however, to give some of them to us in this book, because he was made to feel that the boys and girls of America are entitled to a first-hand knowledge of the history of their great country. And since he holds in his memory one of the choice stories of America's making, — the story of the frontier freighter, — he was finally persuaded to write that story for Americans, young and old. The book itself carries convincing evidence that its author has remembered in vivid detail his early days in old Wisconsin and in the wilds of Wyoming and Nebraska.

A romance of reality is brought to us in *The Bull-whacker.* A boy of old American ancestry is thrust, through a change in his fortunes, out into our frontier life during the picturesque seventies. What happens to him is a series of adventures more truly thrilling than those found in the "movie thrillers." And best of all, these adventures are true.

They all happened during the years just following the driving of the last spike on the first transcontinental railroad. No "spurs," or branches, had yet been laid out from this trunk line. The freighting to the soldier posts and the Indian agencies off the railroad had to be done by primitive methods. The supplies for those holding the frontier line were carried by ox-team trains, which ran on railless roads leading north and south to the outposts of our advancing civilization.

Men of real mettle did this hard and hazardous work. With bullwhips in hand, revolvers on their belts, and rifles within easy reach, they followed the old Cheyenne, Medicine Bow, and Sidney trails into the territory of the untamed redmen. Craggy characters naturally developed out of such service; under a rough exterior the true bullwhacker carried a kindly heart — one full of courage, too, and loyalty always to his friends and to his trust.

The service performed by these frontier freighters was fundamental in the conquest of the plains and the mountains and the deserts. Their bullwhacker's work, though less spectacular was more hazardous than that of the cowboy, and quite as essential.

To most Americans the real story of these ox-team freighters has never been revealed. I must confess that for my own part, though I have felt the heart throbs of the Pioneer West from boyhood, I had never been given a close, human view of bullwhacking until I was privileged to get it from the lips of the author of this book. Then, as I sat with Mr. Hooker in his editorial office in a New York skyscraper, or later in his pleasant home overlooking the Hudson, — where his interested, kindly-spirited wife, who was reared in old Dakota, could prompt his memory, — I began to live through those stirring times.

The result of our conferences was the bringing forth of this volume to add to Pioneer Life Series. It radiates the spirit of the man who lived the life it portrays. It has been illustrated by an artist from the West who has caught and reflected that spirit. And the work has been guided ever with the thought of bringing out a wholesome and truthfully picturesque book for the boys and girls of America.

HOWARD R. DRIGGS

AUTHOR'S FOREWORD

FIFTY years ago this month (May, 1924) as shown in the facsimile page from an account book kept by John Hunton, reproduced on page 163, I was a bullwhacker in Wyoming Territory. That is much more than an average lifetime, according to the latest figures of actuaries; yet I am pleased to state that my recollection of events a half century ago is in most cases quite clear, enabling me to record in this book many of them that I hope will be of interest and benefit, especially to the youth of America who are studying its upbuilding and progress.

Few there are in these days who know what the word "bullwhacker" means, although when hardy men were preparing the way for the present state of civilization west of the Missouri River, the term was as familiar as that of "chauffeur" today. A bullwhacker was a driver of oxen in teams of from five to eight yokes usually attached to two canvas-covered wagons containing freight for outlying army posts or Indian reservations far from railroads.

The work of a bullwhacker was hard in all seasons, but to a young man seeking adventure the hardships and dangers were not always objectionable. Some of those related in the following pages would, I believe, have little attraction for the average youth of today; and what I have included in my experiences on the trails is given mainly with the purpose of making permanent record of a phase of pioneer life that has vanished with the coming of railroads and other development; nevertheless I have tried to make the story entertaining. There is no opportunity in America today for any boy

to follow in my footsteps, for there are no more bull
trains and no more warlike Indians.

To attempt to tell the full story of my adventures on
the old frontier would require at least three volumes the
size of this one, therefore it will, I hope, be understood
that I have touched only a few high spots of the record
in my effort to furnish a volume to meet the requirements
of the publishers — a book to be uniform in size with
the others in the "Pioneer Life Series."

The Bullwhacker contains in revised form a number of
stories from my *Prairie Schooner*, published in 1918 by
Saul Brothers, Inc., of Chicago, which company very
generously waived its copyright.

The timeworn custom of a formal dedication does not
appeal to me for the reason that there are so many dear
friends to choose from. But I am unwilling to allow this
slice of my life to go between covers without some sort
of tribute to the following handful of survivors of the
period covered in the narrative, and who foregather at
times in New York City as an organization under the
title of "The Plainsmen": Edmund Seymour, former
cowboy in Wyoming, now Wall Street banker and presi-
dent of the American Bison Society, New York; Colonel
George W. Stokes, Black Hills pioneer gold miner, New
York; Albert H. Baiseley, bullwhacker on the Santa Fé
Trail, New York; Martin S. Garretson, secretary of the
American Bison Society and scout for that organization,
Clifton, N. J.; Major A. B. Ostrander, early-day soldier
at Wyoming garrisons, New York. Also the Honorable
John Hunton, one-time freighter and my employer in
the seventies, now living happily at Torrington, Wyoming,
in close proximity to the lively scenes of his early life;
Ellis Taylor Peirce ("Bear Tracks"), early-day Black
Hills sheriff, "trail-hound," and terror to road agents

and horse thieves, Hot Springs, South Dakota; Clark B. Stocking, bullwhacker, guide, guard, and all-around frontiersman, Los Angeles, California; and last but by no means least, my wife, erstwhile cowgirl in the Jim River country of old Dakota.

To these dear friends and all others of the frontier days who survive, some of whom participated with me in the stirring events related, I dedicate this book with a feeling of deep affection.

William Francis Hooker

CONTENTS

Contents

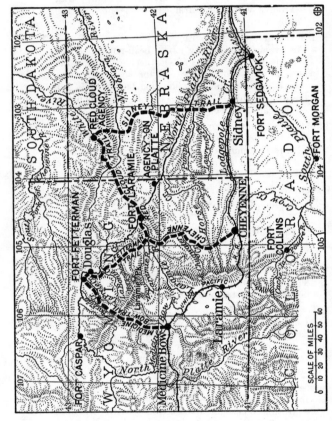

Map showing the principal trails in Wyoming and Nebraska used by freighting bull trains of the seventies.

A wagon train of the seventies stretching out across the plains.

CHAPTER ONE

OLD WISCONSIN TO WYOMING TERRITORY

I WAS born in what was called "Lower Town" in Fond
du Lac, then in the very midst of a nest of sawmills.
"Fondy," as nearly every one called the place, was at
that time almost wholly lost among the rafts of logs
and the great piles of lumber, laths, and shingles. And
now, sixty and more years since I heard the sound, the
whine of the big circular saws, as they cut their way
through the great pine logs, rings in my ears. I can
hear still what happened in the Galloway and Sexsmith
mills when the saw struck a knot, for there was a
whing-ze---z-z-z-z-z-zip! as it slowed down and, cutting
through, resumed the quicker speed, forming a note that
was really sweet music and soothing to my young soul.

My father was at that time an iron molder, a burly,
heavy-fisted, freckled, red-headed man. His father was
a Connecticut Yankee, and his mother, whose maiden
name was Goss, was a mixture of Irish and English.
My mother was a native of England. Her maiden name
was Mary Ann Peacock, and she was born in Yorkshire.

1

My father was born in New York State, and was a direct
descendant of Jonathan Carver, early explorer in northwestern America.

I was born on the 17th of May, 1856, less than a city
block from a big sawmill, and the same distance from
the iron foundry, partly owned by my Uncle John Peacock, the others interested being Alex White and John
Hiner. But Uncle John finally gave up his interest in
the foundry and devoted his time to politics. By the
time I reached the age of eight he had been elected
sheriff of Fond du Lac County. His size alone was
enough to terrify any wrongdoers, for at that time he
weighed over three hundred pounds. He was the eldest
of his father's ten children, and a California "Forty-
niner," having walked both ways across the plains and
mountains. I wear today a ring made from gold he
mined near Sacramento.

Uncle John Peacock had a profound influence upon
my life, but he passed on to the other world without a
suspicion of that fact. Perhaps it was he who mapped
my career for me, or a part of it, at least. Anyway,
when I began to play hookey and devoted most of my
time when so doing to diving off slippery logs in the sawmill district, my mother appealed to him. One day, as I
emerged from the water to dress, the first thing I saw was
my huge uncle, the sheriff, standing in his shirt-sleeves
and confronting me, with my clothes under his arm.

Uncle John had previously been very kind to me,
always had a smile for me, and seemed to be a jolly
good man, as most fat men are. Now, however, I was
amazed not only to be confronted by him, but to discover that his voice had changed to that of a devil
incarnate. His jaw was set and he scowled, and, if I
remember correctly, he said things that I could not very

well include in this tale. As I came timidly up the bank, he seized me and clapped a handcuff on one of my wrists. Then we started for the county jail afoot, and it was a long distance. All the time Uncle John looked straight ahead and squeezed the handcuff that clasped my wrist.

"You are going to jail, young man, and tomorrow the judge will probably send you to prison for life, if he doesn't order your head cut off," my captor shouted more than once.

Of course I was terribly frightened, but somehow I wanted to go to jail. Still, I begged and promised until finally, within sight of the bastile, he took off the cuff and told me to run for my life. I made a bee line for home, but within an hour I was in the street with a gang of boys, boasting over my adventure and expressing regret that Uncle John had not locked me up. Really I felt that I had missed an experience which I believed would glorify me and make me a hero in the eyes of the whole world.

My youthful perspective was askew — no doubt of that. I was under the influence of those tragic Civil War times; but the influence was not all toward evil. I had a good Christian mother. Though she was a member of no church organization, she left nothing undone in her attempts to guide me along the right path of life — a task that she never neglected to the day of her death, hopeless as it always seemed.

My father's principles were likewise high, and he tried to bring me up in the way I should go. He was a firm believer in the use of the rod, in face of constantly accruing evidence of the failure of the system as a corrective as far as I was concerned. Following every such chastisement, I ran away not only from school but from home, sometimes staying away a week. Years before his death, however, when we were pals if ever men were pals, he admitted his mistake. By that time a self-educated man, he had become a member of the legislature — with his son, once regarded by him as absolutely incorrigible, his adviser and at one period his campaign manager and backer.

When I was about eleven years old, my parents moved to Milwaukee. Here an attempt was made to get me to attend a public school, but with no success. Instead I went to work, first as a carrier on the Milwaukee *Sentinel.* After nearly thirty years of varied experiences I was to return and become an editor on this same paper. I also worked as a boy in Milwaukee in several shops — a sash, door, and blind plant, a stave mill, a paint shop, and a furniture store. Finally I became a call boy in the yards of the Chicago and Northwestern Railway.

At the age of fifteen I was earning $30 a month. I soon became a favorite, not only among telegraph operators, train despatchers, and waybill clerks, but also with agents and high officials. Upon the death of my mother, they all took a deeper interest in me. Their concern for my welfare was increased by the fact that my father about this time had the great misfortune to lose a leg in a foundry accident. Being thus disabled, he turned to a lighter kind of work.

Then came a turn in my fortunes which sent me into the frontier life of the West. Friends of my family — railroaders — had gone to work on the new Union Pacific Railroad, and letters from the boys of these neighbors began to rouse the spirit of adventure within me. When it was believed I was affected with the germ of tuberculosis, from which disease my mother had died, I was more than ever determined to get out into the great open spaces. My mother had advised me to do this at the first opportunity, and expressed regret that she had not taken the open-air cure before it was too late.

As a messenger boy it was frequently necessary for me to meet that good man, Marvin Hughitt, then a railroad superintendent. When he heard my story, he not only advised a quick move, but gave me a pass to Council Bluffs, Iowa, with a personal letter to S. H. H. Clark, then manager of the Union Pacific at Omaha, Nebraska. He also gave me a letter addressed "To Whom It May Concern."

In a few weeks I was headed for Wyoming Territory. I ought to add here that when I left home I did so with my father's consent and his blessing, which he pronounced with his hand resting upon my head and with a prayer on his lips.

At the time I left home I weighed about a hundred pounds. I had coal-black hair, which made my thin face seem even paler than it was naturally. This description, however, takes no account of a deep-seated cough and occasional flashes of red on my cheeks. The fear was expressed by friends that I had not soon enough decided to go West.

After paying for one hand bag and a Derringer revolver, which was little better than a popgun, I had $85 in cash, a large sum in those days for a youth of my age.

At Omaha I went directly to the office of Mr. Clark and asked for a pass to Sherman, Wyoming Territory.

"Haven't you any money?" asked Mr. Clark, rather gruffly.

I replied, "Yes, sir; and I will pay my fare, too, although I am a railroad man, if you don't want to give me a pass."

"Railroad *man!*" he exclaimed in a tone that nettled me; but he prevented my saying what I had in mind by turning away, looking out of a window, and adding:

"Well, maybe I'll give you an order for a half-fare ticket."

"Thank you," I said, starting for the door, without noting the merry twinkle in his eyes; "I don't want to be impolite — but I'm no half-fare fellow."

Mr. Clark laughed heartily and said he was trying to see if I had the pluck that I would need in bucking up against the world in one of its roughest spots. Then he most willingly gave me the pass. A pleasant chat followed, during which I told the big railroader that I wanted a railroad-office job, recommending myself, largely on my own confidence, as a good bill clerk. The job was given me. The discovery was made the very first day that all I knew of railroad clerical work was how to copy waybills on a big hand press, with dampened cloths and tissue sheets.

When I had failed as a bill clerk, the agent, impressed doubtless by the letter from Mr. Hughitt, put me with a gang of freight handlers. This proved to be a good thing, temporarily, for it gave me some more money. In the end, however, it was my undoing — also temporarily — because the gang, in unloading a carload of beer from St. Louis, put aside in a derailed box car several kegs of beer for their own use. The result was the discharging of the whole gang.

Over the mountains I went to Cheyenne, really with no plans except to see some of the wild life of that then wild frontier town.

CHAPTER TWO

WHEN I walked out to Camp Carlin at Fort Russell, where the warehouses were located and where the bull trains were loaded for their long treks to the army posts north and northwest of Cheyenne, I was piloted by Nath Williams, John Hunton's wagon boss. For days Nath had posted himself in a big chair in front of Tim Dyer's "Tin Restaurant," opposite McDaniel's hurdy-gurdy in Cheyenne, his purpose being to intercept any bullwhackers or prospective bullwhackers who might emerge from that hell hole so flat broke that they would want to go to work.

The wagon boss on the lookout for prospective bullwhackers.

The truth of the matter is that the Sioux Indians were at that time lifting every scalp they could get action on along the trails to the army posts located on the North Platte River. Some of the bullwhackers naturally were none too anxious to take unnecessary chances in making an honest living, especially when they had money in their pockets and there was so much to see and do in Cheyenne.

When I ran across Williams, I was not emerging from

7

McDaniel's. I had been there, however, but I just then was rounding the corner from Jack Allen's "Gold Room," another place of similar evil import. It was a combination, indeed, of hurdy-gurdy, dance hall, and gambling place — where faro, roulette, twenty-one, and other games were in full swing. I was flat broke, having left my last dollar with the dealer at the faro table.

Nath, who sat propped up in his chair with his feet on the rung, dropped down to the sidewalk when I came along. He greeted me as an old friend would do, although I had never met him before in my life.

The wagon boss wore a big sombrero, brim turned high up in front and fastened to the crown with an ash splinter. He was without coat or suspenders, wearing just a flannel shirt, buckskin trousers, and a pair of boots — no underclothes. Around his slim waist was a big leather belt upon which hung a revolver in a scabbard, and a butcher knife; every loop in the belt contained a cartridge.

Williams introduced himself by inviting me into the barroom, saying as we entered — and very tenderly, too:

"You look as ye hadn't a friend in the hull world — hev ye bin gamblin'?"

I admitted that I had and that I was "busted" higher than a kite, and expressed appreciation of his kindness.

He allowed that it didn't cost anything to be kind, and that while he might not have a reputation for being soft-hearted, he *was* just the same. It made him feel bad when he found a fellow man in my fix.

"You don't look much like a bullwhacker, or as if you ever done a lick o' work in yer life," he went on; "but if you want a job, I've got one for ye whackin' bulls."

I had seen a number of wagon trains strung out across

the plains, and they had fascinated me, but I had never
been wild enough in my imagination to believe that I

A bullwhacker at noonday rest.

should ever have a chance to wield a whip; so Nath
Williams's invitation to go to Camp Carlin with him
was eagerly accepted. And that is where we went after
he had taken me into Tim's famous "Tin Restaurant"
— so called because the dishes were all tin — and filled
my empty stomach with the best in the house.

At the camp we found half a dozen men lying on
their backs under wagons, sleeping, while another was
putting new spokes into a wheel. Shoving his boot into
the stomach of one of the men, Nath Williams shouted:

"Say, Dan, get up and go out to the herd and drive
in the steers for the mess wagon. If ye cain't find all
of 'em, get some others — anyway a pair of leaders and
some wheelers. I'm goin' to train this kid to be a
whacker, you bet!"

It wasn't long before Dan came into camp with eight
head of tough-looking old bulls. He had two more
slim-built bulls that were lively, as most of Hunton's

cattle were, and they kept Dan, who was mounted on a sorrel herd-horse, busy until he had them in the corral made by the wagons.

Then, with the wagon boss as my teacher, I was inducted into the mysteries of bullwhacking.

Taking out the small pins which ran through little holes in the hickory bows and which were held in place by a thin piece of leather from a boot top, I pulled out the bows, threw them on the ground, and then shouldered — on my left shoulder — the heavy ash or pinion yoke, stooping over and picking up in my right hand one of the bows — the one to be worn by the off steer.

Putting the bow pin between my teeth, and with the bow in my right hand, I approached one of the oxen that was pointed out to be my off wheeler.

As I stepped up, the ox took a step backward, and I spoke softly: "Whoa, Jake; don't you know me, old boy? I'm your valet, and here I am with your collar all spick and span just from the laundry."

But Jake smelled my clothes; the odor wasn't familiar. He crooked his neck and tried to dodge me, whereupon Nath Williams said quietly: "Don't run after him; call him the worst name you can think of and look right at him. Get on his nigh side, boy; that's right. Now press him up to'ward the wagon; that's right. Now slip the bow under his neck — rub it a little till he gits acquainted with ye; you're doin' it fine. Now let the yoke drap on top of his neck — easy now — talk to him a little; tell him anything you mind to — he understands better'n ye think he does, the ol' cuss."

So I got the bow, with Jake's neck in it, into the yoke. Nath told me to let the other end of the yoke rest on the ground. Pointing out another bull, Old

Spot, he said, "Now just take along the bow, rub it on his side, speak to him and say, 'Come on, old boy, yer pardner is waitin' fer ye over yonder; don't ye see?'"

Sure enough, after looking me over, Old Spot very solemnly, under my direction, wended his way over to his mate, made a bluff of hooking him in the ribs, and then settled down in just the spot where he belonged. I stepped in and lifted his end of the yoke up on his neck, put the bow under his neck, drew it up until the little holes showed on top of the yoke, slipped in the pegs, drew the leather strings through, and I had a fine yoke of old, seasoned wheel oxen ready for duty.

They stood docilely facing the wagon wheel while one by one I yoked up the rest of the team, Nath Williams repeatedly complimenting me on my behavior. First came the spirited leaders, one of which I was obliged to chase around the corral for quite a time. The fellows under the wagons meanwhile had waked to the fact that there was a show worth watching, and they sat up. Nath yelled at me to smash one of the bulls on the nose with the hickory bow. I obeyed orders with all my strength, turning Mr. Bull from his mad dash toward the corral entrance to the chains that were spread between two wagons. There, while his eyes rolled and he acted crazy, I finally managed to yoke him to his mate.

When I had the rest under yoke and fastened

An old-time whacker.

with the log chains, Nath came up, and, taking the near wheel bull by the horn, marched him and his mate over the tongue of the mess wagon and made them straddle it.

"Now," said my instructor, "take this whip and just throw it out this way at them leaders," slipping the lash along the ground like a snake that uncoiled itself under the belly of the near lead bull. Immediately, in response to this signal and the command, "Haw!" the animal and his mate came around on a circle. After being punched with the whipstock to make him change his course a little, the leader passed slowly in front of the wheel yoke, standing idly and chewing away. When the last yoke had passed just halfway in front of the wheelers, Nath yelled loudly, "Whoa!" All stopped, and Nath told me to step in between the last yoke (called the "pointers"), pick up the dragging log chain, and hook it into the yoke of the wheelers. The tongue of the wagon was now being held aloft by the wheelers, and the team was ready for the trail.

Then we unyoked and yoked up a half dozen times, the last time in a few minutes and with no trouble with the lively near leader. He responded to my commands and submitted without hesitation to having his "collar" put on.

Then Nath took the whip and cracked it. What a noise! It was like a giant Fourth of July firecracker. I was eager to get that instrument into my hands. He swung it several times over his right shoulder before allowing it to pay out over the backs of the team; then we were off. The team started so fast that Nath stepped back and half set the brake to hold the team straight. Then he turned the whip over to me.

Contrary to your expectations that the first time I

swung the long lash over my head and then attempted to pay it out it wound around my neck, nothing of the kind happened. I didn't do that at all in my lessons, but I admit doing it often afterward when my judgment was poor or when the popper, or lash, got caught in a sage bush or cactus plant. In fact, the worst dose I ever gave myself with the whip was three years or more after this time. It was a mighty interesting and an epochal afternoon, if you please. Long before sundown I had yoked, unyoked, and driven in circles and along stretches of the Cheyenne Trail, in sight of Cheyenne, five yoke of John Hunton's bulls attached to a big freight wagon.

When I went to this camp, I had on a dark business suit and a black, narrow-brimmed felt hat, and my gaiters were fairly well shined; but when I returned that evening with Nath Williams to Cheyenne, I looked as though I had spent the afternoon rolling in the dust of the trail. But that didn't matter — hadn't Nath given me an old sombrero and a belt, and equipped me with a Springfield rifle, an old revolver, and a scabbard?

It had taken but one afternoon to make the metamorphosis. I had learned to yoke up a team, and found the bulls almost kitten-like and quickly responsive to my shouts of "Whoa," "Haw," and "Gee." Nath was apparently pleased with his work, for he told Tim Dyer that he had found one man and could start for Fort Laramie the next day if he could pick up three more even half as good. It made me proud, of course, and I couldn't wait for the time to come when we should wheel out of camp and into what was to me the unknown and dangerous north country.

I was impatient, but not for long. That very night three seasoned whackers had squandered their final dollars and had headed for our camp. But we didn't start the next morning, because two more men quit. They had heard from the guard at the entrance of the fort that a company of soldiers had been ordered out to Bear Springs a few miles north to follow the trail of a band of redskins that had taken a few shots at Parrott's mule train. This suggestion of danger made them prefer to stay in town, even if broke.

Nath Williams went back to Tim Dyer's, and I went with him as a decoy to attract any others who might hesitate. It wasn't long before we had rounded up two brothers who said they were from "York State," and had driven oxen there, hauling logs to a sawmill. It took us the rest of the day to break these men in and go back to town again to complete their outfitting and mine.

An old-time whacker, who seemed to take a big interest in me, advised me to buy a whole caddy of plug tobacco, if I could get Nath to advance the money, which he did. It is also clearly set in my memory that I was about the only whacker in the outfit who had a bit of chewing tobacco. When Nath discovered that I was giving it away, he saw to it that the men paid me the regular price for the tobacco. The boys were only too willing to pay; nevertheless, I refused to take money from them unless it was absolutely forced upon me. The result was they were all good friends and took pains to show me how to do things that were new to me. I also bought a pair of gray blankets, some shirts, rough trousers, heavy knee boots, and other needed supplies, with money that Williams gladly advanced.

Fully outfitted as a regular bullwhacker, I was ready to take the trail.

"The big American horse he rode was without doubt stolen."

CHAPTER THREE

FIRST TRIP OVER THE TRAIL

I SHALL never forget my first day and night on the
Cheyenne Trail. The wagons had been loaded several
weeks before I joined up. Nath had been waiting all
this time to gather in a force of whackers. There were
seven or eight old stand-bys he could always depend on,
but at the end of every round trip between Cheyenne
and the northern forts the crews would change much as
they do on ships. The stand-bys were the kind who
were stone deaf when they heard some one repeat the
latest reports about Indian outrages along the trails.
At least, one would think so; for they had nothing to
say that was loud enough for any one passing to hear.
Fact is, they were hungry — starving — to get into a
scrimmage with the reds, and several of them had scores
to settle; for they had been targets for Sioux arrows

more than once, and one or two of them had been hit. How they did hate the Indians!

Always there were men in these outfits who, while outwardly adventurous and anxious to be in the midst of things, were nevertheless troubled with what is known nowadays as a yellow streak. The first sign of an Indian usually found them hunting for cover. But the great majority of the men who found themselves on the frontier at this time were fearless, and I believe every man in our party, as we wheeled into the Cheyenne Trail at four o'clock that May morning in 1873, was sure of a fight with redskins and anxious for it. So we had no cowards with us, and Nath was glad that at least two men had left his employ — one who had some evil reputation as a killer, and the other not only a disturbing element but suspected of being cowardly.

Before the herd was driven in at the crack of day, I was tumbling nervously in my new blankets on the ground, for the news had been given out the night before that if we had any goodbys to say to sweethearts or others, they had better be said. Before sunup next morning, Nath had said, we should be wheeling 'em along over the rolling surface of the plains toward Horse Creek.

My recollection is that we camped at Schwartz's Station that night. It was a long day's work of fourteen miles; but the surface was hard and the trail good, and soon after dark we were around our campfire. I had been in high spirits all day, with my eyes open for anything unusual. Really, I expected to see an Indian loping across the plain almost any minute, although Nath had assured me that the chances were ten to one that I shouldn't see one on the trip, unless there might be a few at the Frenchman's who pretended to be "good," a squaw at Clay's, and maybe a few far back on the hilltops. Just the same, that old revolver and the small Derringer I had in my hip pocket were constantly cocked and ready for action.

I really wanted action, the hotter the better. It must be remembered that I was a youthful adventurer, born and reared partly on the old forest frontier in northern Wisconsin, and that the blood of an ancient and honorable explorer, Jonathan Carver, flowed in my young veins.

When I saw a horseman appear on top of a hill ahead of us and then disappear as if he had been swallowed up by the earth, and the driver ahead of me shouted back, "There's an Indian!" I removed my Springfield, examined it carefully, and honestly prepared for a siege. But in a moment the figure of the horse and his rider came up out of a coulee like a jack-in-the-box, and I saw, even with my untrained eye, that while the rider was not a white man, he was not an Indian warrior. However, he was an Indian, or at least a three-quarter breed, later identified to me by my new companions as one Seminole, whom I was to meet two years later, and who finally died legally at the end of a rope for one of his numerous crimes. So on the first lap of my journey I came face to face with a famous desperado. He disappeared, after walking his horse slowly past our train and greeting Nath with a few pleasant words. He was first of all a horse thief, and the big American horse he rode was without doubt stolen.

You will think that being so near Cheyenne we would have had all the delicacies of the season at our mess; but if you do, you are wrong. We had simple, wholesome bread, bacon, and coffee, some fresh meat, but no fresh vegetables. In the mess wagon I drove there were, for our use later on, several cases of canned corn and a keg of syrup, but no sugar. Sugar was something I saw only once in a bullwhackers' mess, and that was when I had a cargo of brown sugar — two wagon loads — for Red Cloud Agency; and these bags of sugar contained besides sugar many large hard-head boulders the contractors had put in for weight. Of course, we had all the sugar we wanted on that trip. Mr. Hunton was a bountiful provider. We always were well supplied with the necessaries, and sometimes with such luxuries as dried apples.

While at Horse Creek it was determined that I should be the bread maker, this decision being reached by the unanimous vote of the entire force. I had never made a loaf of bread in my life; but my hands were clean, and that, I was told, was the reason I was chosen. But they were soon as dirty and calloused as the next pair, and sometimes I think there was no man on the job who looked dirtier than I did.

I learned to make bread in one lesson. The recipe was simply this: Take the big dishpan, fill it two-thirds full of flour, with a handful of Dooley's baking powder mixed in, dig a hole in the center of it, take the pan to the creek, pour water in the hole, and mix it well. Then put it in the Dutch ovens, after first greasing them with a bacon rind, next put the ovens on the fire, which should be made from the very start with buffalo chips.

I covered the ovens with hot coals until the covers were white-hot, and then removed the covers with a long stick to see that the bread was not burning. It usually did burn a little, and often we ate it before it was more than half baked.

The bacon was fried in the ovens. The grease from it was always saved and used in various ways. For example, at Fort Laramie we found a sack of potatoes on a warehouse landing, and two of the men, regardless of the large brand "U.S." on the sack, pitched it into one of the wagons we had just unloaded. When a sergeant came along and asked what had become of the bag, one of the bullwhackers sent him on a wild-goose chase after a buck soldier, who had "just packed the sack to a point the other side of the parade ground." By the time the sergeant discovered he had been out-witted, the potatoes were in the bull camp, and before the next night most of them had been "French fried" in the grease and eaten.

But we met no hostile Indians on this trip; in fact, I was sorely disappointed when I got back to Cheyenne a few weeks later; but I was to have my curiosity satis-fied later on, more than once, and I am ready to admit that it wasn't what I thought it was going to be — not one half as frightful as I had anticipated. The most annoying thing about it was that I could see arrows shoot into a wagon box but could not for the life of me tell where they came from. The Indians were not often willing to expose themselves to the wicked fire they would receive from Springfields or Winchesters.

When thus attacked from ambush, the old-time bull-

whackers would corral their wagons, unyoke and keep the cattle in the enclosure, and then dash out in the direction of the firing. They were eager for a close-up, always, but they seldom got one. The Indians, being too wary, kept concealed or ready for a quick retreat the moment they saw they were pursued.

No such excitement, however, was given to us on this first freighting adventure of mine. We made the round trip in safety and were soon back at old Cheyenne ready to take on another cargo of goods for the soldier posts on the North Platte.

The bulls refreshing themselves after a long drive.

CHAPTER FOUR

FROM TENDERFOOT TO PLAINSMAN

FOR the first few weeks I drove the mess wagon, the last in the train. It took pretty hard work to keep from lagging behind; but fear that an arrow might put an end to all my adventures kept me from getting very far in the rear. When my team did show signs of weakening and the space began to increase between me and the man next ahead, Williams would come riding back on his horse and with a big whip help me whack the team into a livelier gait.

All the time I had my Springfield hanging in leather loops on the side of my wagon box, and more than once the first week out I removed it and carried it over my shoulder, especially at spots where the surface was hard and the team moved along without much urging. Every time we entered a creek bottom where there was brush, I was anxious for an Indian to show just a single feather, so that I could prove to those fellows that I was not afraid — especially the two Yanks from "York State," who were the victims of many pranks on the part of the

old bullwhackers. These two Yanks soon became expert
at the business, and in a very short time demonstrated
that they were not the kind to run when shot at from
ambush.

The customary jokes were played for my benefit, but I
had the good sense to take them as they were given; so
I soon established myself in the good graces of all hands.
Nath Williams was open in his expressions of pride in
me, for he said that several of the boys we found under
the wagons that day at Camp Carlin had sniffed and said,
"Dude — no good." They saw only my good clothes.

It would have been an easy matter to make a failure
as a bullwhacker if I had been lacking in a certain
amount of youthful common sense. My first experiences
with men, also, as a call boy in a railroad terminal,
helped me a great deal. Then it was my duty to pound
on a conductor's or an engineer's door and stay there
until I was sure that he was awake and would report
for duty. Some of these men were rough and swore at
me. They would tell me to shut up, or get out, or go to
Hades; but my boss at the telegraph key had told me
not to mind what they said, for they didn't mean it.
And true enough, I soon knew that all the men in the
railway yards were my friends.

When I found myself at the campfire or on the trail
with another class of transportation men who were
many degrees rougher in their ways, I was prepared
and gave little notice to things that might otherwise
have been unpleasant. I was one of them in the fullest
degree, never picking a quarrel, but always defending
myself when I considered I was being badly treated.
And when there were signs of danger ahead I made it
my business to occupy a conspicuous place, never showing the white feather.

Early in my experience on the trail I drove a team that was placed in the train between two other teams, driven by two brothers. These brothers wanted to shift places so that they might be together; but I refused to trade, saying I intended to hold my place unless ordered out of it by the wagon boss, who at the time had gone ahead for a day with another wagon train. They then tried to crowd me out, and finally the elder of the two came back and struck me with his whip. I put on my brakes and stopped. The man behind took my place in the line and held it until the boss returned. I said nothing, but when we strung out the day following, the boss came back on his mule and asked if I wasn't out of my place, and I admitted that I was.

"But why?" he asked.

I said, "Ask Sim."

He asked Sim, and Sim lied, saying I couldn't keep up and that he (Sim) passed me.

Then some one told the boss about the elder brother hitting me with the whip. When he asked me about it, I refused to say a word. The two brothers were worried; a man in the outfit told them they had good reason to be, because he was sure that I had a trump card up my sleeve and that there was lead in it, although I had said not a word.

The result was that the men in the train had concluded that I was able to take care of myself and that I would do it. One of these brothers afterward became a famous desperado and belonged to the Jackson's Hole gang of Union Pacific train robbers.

The men of that time admired a man who stood squarely for his rights, but they despised a whiner. I never whined or complained, and kept my own counsel. My silence was ominous, and it was admired.

What I had I divided, even my money when the other fellow had none. My tobacco was theirs, and if I had picked up at the end of a trail a dainty and put it in my jockey box, I never hid myself away to eat it, but brought it out and divided. When I played cards I never disputed, but quit the game if it became a wrangle. I was handy with a needle and could, after a few lessons, braid a whip, and I not only sewed patches on Nath Williams's trousers, but one noonday surprised the night herder by taking his trousers out of the wagon in which he slept and thoroughly repairing them while the rest dozed under the wagons out of the desert sun. I was often asked to braid a popper into a whip, and never refused. It was the small things — the courtesies — that counted there as they do here and everywhere. I tried hard to play the game fairly and squarely.

One of the last things my father said to me when I left home was to be square and honorable in my dealings with my employers and my fellow workers, but to stand firmly and even fight for my rights when I knew I was right, to select good companions, make friends whenever possible, and to fight for them, too, if necessary. I respected that advice, and ever since then I have tried to pass it on in word and deed to the men and boys who have worked under my direction.

The mess wagon finally descended in regular order to another young man who entered the bullwhacking profession in much the same manner that I did, and I was given the lead team in the second section of the train. This was an important post, for the reason that it required skill to "gee" a team off the trail and swing it around back almost at a right angle to the trail and make the right contour for the wagon corral, of which my two wagons formed a key: It was a difficult job sometimes, because the moment the whacker threw the whip at his near lead bull and told him to "gee," the

Unyoking the bulls.

whole team knew what it meant — going into camp. They were naturally wild to do that part of the day's work, and would run away with four tons of freight unless the teamster knew how to turn the trick and keep them properly strung out and going till it was time to set the brakes and plant the wagons in place.

To see a big train go into camp was a great sight. Every one, including the bulls, was under more or less excitement, hungry and in a hurry; the bulls were thirsty, of course, and if there was water within a mile of camp, the moment the yoke was dropped from a bull's neck he was headed, on a trot, for the creek or river, into which he would wade and stand belly deep to cool his overheated flesh. Sometimes, at a creek, we would have to go far above where the cattle went into the water to get our supply; and we had to be lively about it, too, for they moved quickly, seeking out the tenderest grass shoots and coolest places. Usually no herder went with the bulls until after the meal was served; then he mounted his horse and began to round them up, especially if the stay was to be short, so that they would be handy when the boss was ready to hook up.

At night the cattle were close herded, always by one man, unless the Indians were bothering. At such times Williams and perhaps one or two others would be perched on a knoll with an eye open and an ear and nose keen for unusual sounds or smells — for smells counted. A real old-timer among the bullwhackers who couldn't smell Injuns wasn't considered all he should be. Usually the herd horses got the first whiff of an Indian camp — a smoky, burnt-leathery smell is the only way I can describe it.

"'If you squeal on me, they won't get me; but, boy, I'll get
you.'"

CHAPTER FIVE

MEETING A NOTORIOUS OUTLAW

FOR a few weeks I night-herded for the Charley Clay
outfit, which had contracts to haul freight to Red Cloud
Agency and Camp Robinson, both situated on White
Clay River, or Creek, in Nebraska. The only difference
in the freight hauled was that Camp Robinson got
shelled corn in sacks, and the Indians at Red Cloud got
sugar, bacon, and blankets, sent by Uncle Sam in pay-
ment for the territory south of the North Platte.

Before I reached the White River country I had surrendered the night-herding job to another and was
again whacking a seven-yoke team of splendid bulls.
A few of these understood the English language, as it
was spoken by a bullwhacker, better than any bulls I
had ever handled. Some of them, seeing me coming out
into the corral with my yoke or bow, would come to me;
others would come at call. They could travel like

Kentucky thoroughbreds, and finally won a place where they belonged — in the lead of one section of the train.

But I am going to tell you something about night-herding bulls — not how much I admired my team, though it will do no harm to tell you that some bulls in both Hunton's and Clay's outfits were more intelligent and more tractable than many horses or mules, and that some of us were very proud of our cattle and treated them accordingly. For example, on at least one occasion, while with Clay, I refused to lash my team in a sandy place after it had made one honest effort to move the wagon.

"Swing 'em off again, Bill," shouted the assistant wagon boss, who rode up on a big mule, "and throw the whip into 'em; they can make it all right."

"No, sir!" I replied. "I know this team; I have been over this trail before, and when we reached this spot the other trip we doubled up. I'm not going to make another attempt."

Mr. Clay was with the outfit, as he usually was, and he was appealed to by the assistant wagon boss. The result was that Clay came up and, after looking over the situation, smiled and said, "Bring up the next team, and repeat all along the line."

With fourteen yoke, and sand nearly to the hubs, we walked through with ease, and there was much less delay than there would have been had we put our teams to the severest test and worried them with the whip. Clay watched his chance to speak to me alone later on and praised my judgment, although he said I had possibly made an enemy of the assistant wagon boss — which I had, but only temporarily.

Usually there were long waits at Cheyenne, Sidney, and Medicine Bow, where we got our cargoes of freight.

It was while at Cheyenne that I had begun my experience as a night-herder. We were camped just north of the town close to what is now a park-like section, and the grazing was naturally very poor; so it was necessary for me to take the bulls two or three miles farther out, and work them along slowly during the night, keeping them together and seeing that they had plenty of good grass. During the daytime they also were herded by one man, and after the first night they were driven in only every two days to be checked up by Mr. Clay or a representative, to see that the herders were on the job and not losing the stock.

It was on one of these mornings that the boss himself discovered that I was short one bull. Of course it was my job to go back to the range and not show up until I found the missing animal. I had my breakfast first, and then mounted my horse and dashed over a rise in the ground near by and down a steep incline into a coulee, the other side of which was about a mile away.

Just as I topped the hill I saw a horseman coming down the other grade at a stumbling gait. He saw me at the same moment, and I noted that he removed from the loop around the horn of his saddle a carbine and began to belabor his exhausted horse. He had left the trail and was coming my way. When he was within range, I saw that the carbine, held in one hand, was pointed straight at me. Still, for some unknown reason, I did not surmise that I was being held up or that the horseman was other than a friendly herder or traveler. In a moment he was within a few rods of me.

I stood perfectly still as I recognized him with a smile. He was a tough-looking customer, filthy-dirty, hair hanging far down his back, and face covered with

straggling beard. As he stopped he held his gun on a
line with my head and said, "Do you know me?"

"Sure," I replied without hesitation or the least
particle of fear. "Sure I know you; you're Persimmons
Bill. I saw you last year at Hunton's place near
Fetterman."

He laughed at what he took to be my bravado, but
which was, in truth, nothing of the kind. As I had
never done him an injury, I had absolute confidence he
would have no score to settle with me; so I felt perfectly
safe.

"Well," he continued, "I remember you; you're a
Bill, too, — Skinny Bill, eh?"

I admitted that the boys sometimes called me
"Skinny," and laughed.

"What are you doing here?" he asked. "Hunting for
a lost bull, eh? How far is it to town?"

I told him that he was within a few yards of a spot
where he could get a good squint at Cheyenne.

This made him whirl his horse around and start for
the hill I indicated. Then he changed his mind and,
looking me square in the face, said: "Can I trust you
to do something for me? I'm nearly starved to death.
I rode this hoss from Fort Laramie since yesterday
afternoon, and hain't had a bite. Who are you working
for?"

"I'm with the Clay outfit. We are camped just over
yonder. What do you want me to do — get you something to eat?"

With a string of oaths he said, "You've guessed right.
And let me tell ye something, Skinny: if you squeal
on me, they won't get me, for I'll be a long way from
here before they can start; but, boy, I'll get *you*."

So I promised to get him some grub, and he loped

back to the other side of the coulee to await my return. He wanted to have a good start, provided I reported his presence. But I didn't; I simply rode to the mess wagon and, never dismounting, reached over into the bread box, took out a whole pone and grabbed about two pounds of raw bacon, putting them both inside my shirt and next my flesh, and leisurely walked my horse to the hill and across the coulee, where sat Persimmons Bill on his big American horse that bore the uncanceled "U.S." Beside him was my lost bull, which he had discovered when he had mounted the highest piece of land he could find to see whether I was keeping my word.

I drove the old bull into camp, and reported to the day herder. Before rolling up in my blanket under a wagon, I sat around awhile and chatted with two or three men who had stayed in camp. One of these had been a pretty good pal. To him, under a pledge of secrecy, I told about Bill. He allowed that I was several kinds of a fool, because there were a half-dozen rewards out for Bill, aggregating I have forgotten how much; but he promised to keep the secret, and I believed him.

About an hour later, after I had gone to sleep, a posse of twelve or fifteen horsemen rode into our corral and yanked me out of my blankets. I was tall and gaunt, with my hair, as long as a girl's, hanging down my back. Also, I was barefooted, and was wearing only a shirt and a pair of buckskin trousers. One of the posse had me by the nape of the neck before I was on my feet, and the conversation, leaving out the oaths, ran something like this:

"What's your name?"

I gave it, fearfully.

"Why didn't you come in town and report to the sheriff that you had seen Persimmons Bill? Why did

"One of the posse asked: 'What shall we do with this kid?'"

you feed that murderer, horse thief, and robber instead of turning him over to the law?''

I denied that I had fed him, and said I had simply come into camp and told my friend that I had seen Bill, where he was, and so forth. It looked like a case of life or death for me, and as I was in perfect ignorance of any reward while I was talking to Persimmons Bill, I did not think I was doing such a bad morning's work. I did know that he was a bad character, that he had killed several men, and that he was a reputed horse thief. He had been in our camp near Fetterman, and no one mentioned anything about turning him over to the law.

I was conscientious in all this. I believed at that time of my life that Bill's quarrel with society was none of my affair anyway, and I was doing what many others had done. In fact, there probably wasn't another man in the Clay outfit, except the one who did report the case, who would have done differently. Men of our calling had a habit of attending strictly to their own affairs, and a squealer was looked upon as worse than a criminal.

Then one of the posse asked: "What shall we do with this kid?"

"Turn up a wagon tongue and hang him," shouted another.

"Oh, no, that wouldn't ever do," said a third; "he didn't know Bill was wanted. He's just an ignorant boy, and I don't care whether he fed him or not; let's take the trail."

Before I could make a move to get back under the wagon, they had put spurs to their fine horses and were off to the north. I am not stretching it a bit when I say that my legs shook and that I slept no more that day. Also, when the man who did report the presence of Persimmons Bill in sight of Cheyenne returned to the Clay camp, he found no friends that I can remember, and before we pulled out for the north he had departed.

I afterward learned that the posse was made up of a sheriff's force of deputies and several well-known ranchmen and others who happened to be in Cheyenne at the time. I have often wondered since I began to relate this exciting event of my boyhood whether there was a man in that fine body of horsemen named Van Tassel. He is living in Cheyenne, still a great cattle rancher and capitalist, and he knew me as a bullwhacker.

Of course, it was wrong to befriend Persimmons Bill; but has it occurred to you that if I had not done so, I might not be here to tell you this story? It is highly probable that he might have lain in wait for me, as he did for the stages that later on took the Argonauts to the Black Hills. If he had, I might have been so filled with lead that my friends would not have recognized me. I had no desire to be made food for the coyotes. But even now I cannot say that I acted as I did from any fear of the consequences had I reported him to the authorities. I did what I did, because that was the best judgment I had at that stage of my life.

I night-herded in some pretty tight places. Some nights there was no moon, all as dark as pitch; some brought storms, when the cattle tried to scatter and fell into deep holes. But I never permanently lost a single bull.

On one occasion a regular norther blew across the plains while I was taking the bulls to their feeding ground, great hailstones came down upon my head and upon the head and back of my horse, and he was almost unmanageable. The cattle ran in every direction, and

I soon found myself in the midst of them. The hailstones were cracking their heads, too.

Finally, I managed to get the saddle off my horse and put it over my head, hanging on to my bridle while the horse swung around me and nearly pulled me off my feet. After the storm several men came out from camp, and in a short time we had the herd quietly feeding, although we were nearly frozen to death. This storm, as I remember, occurred in midsummer. It was a very unusual one in Wyoming.

Frequently the cattle, while thoroughly broken and tamed by hard work, became excited to the point of stampeding. At such times they would break into a run, usually in the same direction, especially when they smelled burning leather or when they knew a wolf was close at hand. It was then that I had my hands full and a large job cut out to get them either bedded down or feeding.

Usually night-herding was a lonely and uneventful vigil. There was, at certain times, every reason to expect an attack from Indians. This was enough to keep almost any one from violating a rigid rule, which was not to go to sleep under any circumstances. But I violated that rule many times, once to awaken and find day breaking and not a bull in sight, although when I fell asleep they were closely bedded before me. Before the boss discovered what had happened, I had the herd headed for the wagon corral and it was broad day, which fact made the "old man" suspicious. But as I had lost none of the stock, the matter was turned off with a few winks and blinks and insinuations to the effect that I must enjoy long hours.

The rule was to turn the bulls into camp at the first appearance of daylight. More often the bullwhackers

Morning at the bullwhackers' camp.

took issue with my judgment, asserting that it was too early; but if there was a timepiece in any bull outfit that I was ever with, I do not remember it. Clay, Hunton, Williams, and other bosses no doubt had them; but a bullwhacker — never. We kept time by the sun.

Unlike the present-day flyers, bull trains did not run on schedules, although there was a pretense of regularity about the day's routine, which was about as follows:

At break of day the night-herder who had been out with the bulls all night — it is always daybreak to him, whether three o'clock or five — drives his herd into the corral, usually singing some refrain of his own composition, but always having for its motive the same that animates the pestiferous alarm clock set by a master to disturb the slumber of a tired servant. However, a half hour before the herder appears, the cook and his helper, both bullwhackers, doing their turn of a week, have been on the job with the coffee and bacon, and as soon as the herder sounds his first note, the cook takes up the song, which is, perhaps:

> Bacon in the pan,
>   Coffee in the pot;
> Get up and get it —
>   Get it while it's hot.

And then, and it is always so, some of the lively stock, as it approaches the corral, takes the notion that there is some nice sweet buffalo bunch grass to the rear that looks better than a day's work, and there is a bolt often approaching a stampede. Curses? You never heard the like, for the wagon boss and an assistant are already in their saddles helping the herder. If you tried to sleep just a minute longer, it would be impossible; therefore you roll out from your bed on the ground, fold up your blankets, tie them with a strap, and throw them on your trail wagon.

Coffee and bacon are swallowed in haste, and if you are like the majority, you grab a piece of bacon and a chunk of bread, bang them together into a huge sandwich, and put them in the jockey box of your wagon for a lunch at eight or nine o'clock. This done, the bullwhacker is ready to string out his team and strike out on the trail.

"Beautifully antlered elk, drifting with the wind, marched past."

CHAPTER SIX

ON THE MEDICINE BOW TRAIL

Much of my freighting experience was on the old trail leading from Medicine Bow station on the Union Pacific Railroad across the plains north to Fort Fetterman. The streams and the mountains here are all of the same name — for we ford the Big Medicine River and two smaller Medicine tributaries; we climb the Medicine Bow breaknecks, and out, finally, upon the great Medicine Bow plateaus that slope down into La Prele Creek, and thence to the valley of the North Platte.

Medicine Bow was everywhere. It was all Medicine Bow, including the seldom traveled trail — all made permanently famous by Owen Wister in his *Virginian*, although his knowledge of the Medicine Bow country was gained more than a decade and a half after my experiences in that lovely country. Wister was there when school teachers who had come to teach the young idea how to shoot listened to the brave words of the cowboy. He found there also not a few farmers who had sought out the fertile valleys, which we of earlier times looked upon as deserts. This was largely because we had listened to the propaganda of fur companies. They were not interested in having the rich valleys and the waving grass of the uplands invaded by the plow and the threshing machine or herds of cattle.

The cattlemen too — after my time — came and resented the appearance on the scene of the agriculturist. But none of us, no matter what interests we represented, took much note of what fate was in store for the Indians. They spent their time in the Medicine Bow region chasing the antelope, which they found there in droves of tens of thousands. Now and then for diversion they would lift a white man's scalp.

But let us drive our big Bain, Shuttler, Murphy, and other wagons up to the doors of the freight cars and load the bacon and the flour and the sacked corn and get away across the wind-swept plains.

It all happened too long ago for me now to remember with any degree of accuracy where we camped one day or another. But if I live to be as old as Methuselah, I shall never forget that we traveled for three days with a great mountain in clear outline on our left. Though we moved along at a good gait on the hard, flat surface, we seemed never to be able to get away from the great blue peak. In looking at a map of Wyoming now, I do not find Diamond Peak; but it is there, perhaps under another name, not shown, for there is no likelihood that it has disappeared. And it is so indelibly printed on my brain that as I write it looms into view as perfectly as it did in those days of the early seventies.

And how the wind did blow, those three summer days!

Clouds of dust that rose on our right must have looked at a distance like a great prairie fire. Canvas covers were flapping like thunder, whips were cracking, and the heads of a couple of hundred of John Hunton's bulls were straining in their yokes.

Let us stop for dinner at noon, out on this perfectly flat plain. Let us build a fire of buffalo chips and a few small sticks of wood, which the boys picked up at "the Bow" and strapped together in a bundle.

A frying pan to me was an appetizer — just the sight of one made me hungry. When I saw a half dozen of them come out, and then a slab of unsacked back bacon thrown on the tailgate of a wagon drawn close to the fire, my mouth began to water. But when the coffee in several big pots began to boil and steam, and they were lifted off with long sticks, when the tin cups and tin plates and knives and forks were dumped out on the ground, and the big pones of bread, looking like loaves of German rye, that were baked the night before when we had plenty of wood, were brought out, then my mouth did water.

No matter how delicate you may be in the matter of eating, I believe if you had been there, you would have been as ravenous as the rest of us. You would have relished every mouthful you ate. Although this was a summer day, with a bright sun shining overhead, still there was a chill in the heavy wind that was scudding across the big sweep of prairie. This added an appetizer to the natural hunger resulting from the work of a long drive and almost constant throwing of a heavy whip upon the flanks of seven yoke of bulls.

While we are eating, the bulls are having their nooning, always a period of a couple of hours at least. This gave them time to nibble the rich grasses and an opportunity to lie down and chew the cud. The bulls had to have rest, and for that reason, and that alone, the bullwhackers had one. Nevertheless, they did not always improve the chance as they should. Several had their own ponies tied behind their wagons, and it was their practice in the game country to dash off a few miles and look for an antelope, a sage grouse, a coyote, or anything else in the way of game. Others sat under the wagons, with the tailboard of a wagon as a table, and played freezeout, either for money or plug tobacco. Still others took a nap.

It took several days to cross the Medicine Bow plains and reach the foothills of the mountains of the same name. Every camp was about the same, except that at some places our menu was varied with antelope steak or a well-parboiled sage hen or two, some of the boys having had luck in their hunting.

Along this trail there were bands of elk, lots of them, but we did not sight them this particular season. Later on, however, in winter, as I was passing over the range between Fetterman and "the Bow" aboard a cayuse, I was caught in a blizzard. I had built a small fire, put my arm through the bridle reins, and squatted down to toast my almost frozen fingers, when suddenly I heard a whistle, sharp and clear.

The wind was blowing a gale from the northwest, and as I looked up I saw traveling slowly before it some dozens of beautifully antlered elk, their hind quarters humped and the snow piled upon their backs as they marched on past me in the direction the wind was blowing. I was not looking for elk; therefore my Winchester, slung across my saddle, remained where it was, and the herd went on about its business of keeping backs to the blizzard, presumably until the storm ceased, while I spent the next day or two in following the stream I took to be one of the "Little Medicines," until finally I discovered the trail that took me in a few hours to "the Bow" and a warm fire.

Up in the foothills Uncle Sam had strung a few heavy pine logs across a chasm that must have had a depth of five hundred feet, and this narrow structure was called a bridge. However, as it covered only a gash in the earth about thirty feet in width, there was no need of anything to brace it; so it was a suspension log bridge. Over it went our wagon train, although it was at first difficult to get the leaders of nearly every team in the outfit to take the first step. After that all went smoothly, and there were no mishaps; but it was necessary for the bullwhackers to walk beside their teams going over, and I distinctly remember that there was not more than a foot of space to walk in, and that if the bull upon whose back I placed my hand had become frightened and side-stepped six inches, I would have careened to the rocky bottom of the chasm.

I afterward passed over this unique bridge with a

rum-runner named Dunn. He had a ten-gallon keg of whisky on a "democrat wagon" and very willingly took me "for company," as he said, to Fort Laramie via Fort Fetterman; he needed a guide, and as I knew the trails perfectly, I took him, not into the post at Fort Fetterman, but around it to La Bonte Creek, thence east, leaving him at Fort Laramie. I went on down to the Chugwater, where I joined the Charley Clay outfit.

In those days white men, with black hearts, sold liquor to the Indians, and this man was one of that stripe, though he was, as I discovered while with him as his guide and companion, a man of a good family in New England, and had a fairly good education. In my case it was either go with this rum-runner or make the trip alone. I had to meet the Clay outfit.

In our freighting trip from "the Bow" to Fetterman, we had to wind around the difficult and dangerous mountain "breaknecks"—trails about half dug in the sides of the mountains, where we looked down several hundred feet upon the tops of the trees. Sometimes when these trails were so crooked that my lead bulls would be out of sight, I was sure they would get excited and drag everything over into the valley; but the bulls seemed to know the necessity of careful stepping, and there were no mishaps—not this trip. I heard a year or so later that a team did plunge into the abyss, taking two wagons and a cargo with them, and that it fell where it was impossible to recover anything.

What a magnificent camp we had in these mountains the first days! Fast-running streams seemed to be everywhere, dashing over rocks here and there in pretty waterfalls, and supplying the best water we had had to drink since leaving "the Bow." There were numerous little natural parks, some very tall grass, lots of aspen and young cottonwoods and box elders forming shady nooks in which we built our temporary camps. Trout darted out of the streams everywhere, and as we had plenty of fishing tackle, our menu of bacon and venison was improved for several days, for we had all the fish we wanted, and more.

Here in the midst of the mountains were many things to attract the eye of a youngster ever on the lookout for something unusual, and one that seemed the most wonderful to me at the time was the wreck caused by a snowslide of the previous winter. Apparently no one had been over the trail ahead of us this season, for the great rocks and trees covered the trail, and we were obliged to spend many hours in making a new path, partly around the old one, throwing aside logs by "snaking" them with teams of bulls and the use of several heavy log chains.

I found, also, a small cabin quite a distance off the trail. It showed signs of having been inhabited quite recently, for there were in and near it pieces of deerskin, bones, fresh ashes, and footprints. The cabin was hardly worthy of the name, though it had a small fireplace, was roofed over, and very comfortable, but hastily thrown together by some one who either had nothing but a hatchet or who was too lazy to cut the ends off his logs. I found the mysterious hiding place — for that is what it proved to be — while trying to find a path to a point below a small waterfall.

At Fetterman a few weeks later I told Black Jack, the mail carrier, of my discovery. He was deeply interested and told me that my find was mighty important, because he knew that a couple of "road agents" were in the hills somewhere, and he had been on the lookout for them for several months. Evidently, he said, they were camped in there awaiting an opportunity to take him unawares and rob him. Next trip, he said, he would be on guard more than ever, especially in this part of the mountain range.

I never heard whether Black Jack had any adventure with these robbers or not, although I do know that for two winters after this time he carried the mail regularly over great drifts, in blizzards of the most terrible kind. He always landed safely at either end of the trail, unfrozen and with his mail sack intact.

I think we were in the mountains about four days this trip, although, as related in another chapter, I spent about a month there one winter, being unable to move an inch without shoveling.

Out of the north mouth of the valley we came upon a great hogback or ridge upon which the trail followed for many miles, thus avoiding heavy grades and the necessary bridging of creeks down below, until we reached the headwaters of La Prele Creek, which flows on down to Fort Fetterman perhaps thirty-five or forty miles to the north, on the North Platte River. The trail passed to the west of the now famous natural bridge, across which at about this time John Hunton, owner of our outfit, rode on his horse.

In October, 1921, I went with Mr. Hunton to this picturesque spot and had our pictures taken, while two sportsmen from a near-by city cast their lines into the stream that passes under the great arch and brought forth more than one trout weighing a full pound. We spent some hours in wending our way through the gnarled underbrush of old La Prele Creek, and I tried to imagine myself back in days long past, listening to discover the possible presence of an Indian band! But all I heard was the tooting of several auto horns, and finally there came into view six cars containing gayly dressed ladies out for a Sunday visit to the natural bridge, only an hour from their homes in Douglas. And then I tried to blot them out of the scene, and vision only the wild days of the early seventies, but I could not; so we cranked up our Ford and sped away between the wire fences, bordering solid, well-made roads, to a point where we found a red mark of weeds climbing over the rolling hills above the irrigation ditches and growing crops.   There we stopped and recognized the old Medicine Bow Trail over which we had so many times toiled and sweated, shouted, and used bad language, and we were both sad.

Then we visited, on another day, the site of Mr. Hunton's cabin, built in 1874 just inside the United States reservation, taking down several sections of wire fence here and there in order to get to the spot, which we located by first finding a few riffles of the creek which I remembered were directly opposite the log house.   In this way we were able to pace off the space occupied by the log station and the blacksmith shop and charcoal kiln adjoining.   Here, at various times, occurred many exciting events, some of which are related elsewhere. About four miles north from this camp of Hunton's was the old Oregon Trail crossing of La Prele not far from the entrance up a short hill to Fort Fetterman.

The journey from "the Bow" ended at the big adobe warehouses in the fort, where our cargoes were deposited, and then there was a rest for both men and bulls.   The latter were taken up the creek to good feeding ground and turned loose, usually with some one watching to see that the Indians did not stampede them across the Platte.   On one occasion, when Mr. Hunton thought there were no Indians in the vicinity because they had been reported active at other points, they swept down one bright summer morning, rounded up thirty head of his finest steers (work bulls), and taking them to a ford in the river drove them away to the north.   This was a severe loss, for work bulls were hard to find, not so easy to buy, and it took time to break range cattle.

CHAPTER SEVEN

AROUND OLD FORT
FETTERMAN

FORT FETTERMAN, the end of
both the Medicine Bow Trail
and one branch of the Cheyenne Trail, was the scene of
some rather unpleasant experiences for the frontier
freighters. To speak frankly,
these hardy, unshaven wielders
of the bullwhip did not get
along very smoothly with the trim army officers. The
fault probably was on both sides, though I must say
in fairness that the army officer who was responsible
for discipline had much to put up with in dealing with
men used to having their own free, wild way.

There were two bars in Tillotson's store at Fort
Fetterman — one for the officers, the other for white
citizens and buck soldiers. A whitewashed line marked
the boundary. To get across it meant a trip to the
guardhouse. The officers didn't care to rub elbows with
uncouth bullwhackers, no matter if these were drivers
of the ox-team outfits, often risking their lives to haul
supplies to these same officers out in the wilds. At this
distant period, however, it doesn't seem so serious a
slight as it did then.

There was a decided difference in appearance between
the bullwhacker and the graduate from West Point.
Clean-shaven, neatly dressed Major Kane, for instance,
did not greatly resemble Sim Waln, with his shaggy hair
and beard, elkskin breeches, greasy sombrero, buckskin

48

shirt, belt sagging from the weight of two revolvers and a supply of cartridges, and a butcher knife with a ten-inch blade. The bullwhacker had the advantage of being more picturesque, perhaps; but the marked differences in appearance, added to army distinctions, kept the two types of men, even though both were doing frontier service, far apart.

A kind of feud was gradually developed. The bull-whackers inwardly resented being looked upon as inferiors, and did many things at times to provoke the military men. The officers at times became exasperated and meted out punishment with a harsh hand. These same officers nearly all drank hard liquor — some of them excessively; but let them catch a bullwhacker making a crooked step — hardly a stagger — as he emerged from Tillotson's store, and it would mean a trip to the guardhouse.

At that time there was no semblance of civil law north of Medicine Bow. The military out in the Wyoming wilds in those frontier days was all-powerful. There was none other than the belligerent-looking bullwhacker for the officers to exercise their authority upon, and they took occasion at the least provocation to exercise it.

But the hard feelings growing out of the feud have passed away. One of the men, at least, who whacked bulls for John Hunton in those long-ago days takes this opportunity to forgive Major Kane for the indignity heaped upon the said bullwhacker when, as officer of the day, the major ordered him thrown into the guard-house. The offense was that he had crossed a forbidden spot of the parade ground to get a look at the first Gat-ling gun ever sent west of the muddy Missouri. The punishment was three days in jail, on a diet of sour bread and of plain water from La Prele Creek. A mys-

terious hand pushed this hard fare in a tin receptacle
through a small aperture at the bottom of a heavily
barred door.

Other boys of our outfit suffered similar severe
punishments. One of them, for some offense, was tied
"spread eagle" on top of a cannon; that is, back down,
arms and legs outstretched and roped, face to the sun.
He got a kind of revenge for this and other indignities
heaped on him by striking in rather a mean way at the
pride of an unpopular commanding officer. One night,
just before a big parade was to be staged, this bullwhacker and another man at the post trimmed the tail
of the officer's charger in fantastic fashion.

The wrath of the general, when he found his favorite
horse so barbered, was ominous. He offered $500 reward
for the delivery and conviction of the perpetrators of
the deed, but they were not discovered. The incident
caused a canceling of the parade.

The enmity between bullwhackers and soldiers at one
time came near to flaming out into open conflict. A
number of the freighters, feeling that they had been
deeply wronged by the military leaders, finally met one
night up La Prele Creek and plotted, Indian fashion, to
get revenge. Among the various reprisals they decided
on were these: the first officer caught alone away from
the fort was to be captured, tied to a tree, and flogged;
the stacks of hay to the south of the fort were to be
burned; any Indians who chanced that way were to be
encouraged to stampede the mule herd of the soldiers.
In a word, a secret war was to be waged.

But a sober second judgment seemed to hold the bullwhackers in check. The soldiers and the freighters
glared at each other for some years, but they did not
come to any serious clashes.

The bitterness engendered was swept away somewhat, it is said, when General Custer visited Fetterman. He kept on friendly terms with the bullwhackers, one day inviting them and the other civilians to cross the white-washed line and have a drink with him. He had come to Fort Fetterman, I was told, to make preparation for the Sioux campaign that resulted in his death in June, 1876. Harmony there must be, he felt, if the work of subduing the Indians was to be carried to a successful conclusion.

The Sioux and other Indians were then making their last stand for their best hunting grounds — Absaraka, the land lying on the eastern slopes of the Rockies, in Wyoming and the Montana country. This was then all a wild, unranged, untilled expanse of sage and grassy plains and hills, crossed by fast-flowing streams. Deer, antelopes, beavers, bears, wildcats, wolves, coyotes, mountain lions, and other game still roamed at will. A few small, straggling buffalo herds were still to be seen on these upland plains, but the great buffalo range was farther down on the Platte and the Republican rivers, and in Kansas.

In their fight to keep the whites off their last hunting reserve, the Indians kept up their attacks whenever they could get an advantage. They kept rather shy of Fort Fetterman, but they sometimes would get close enough to put a bullet or an arrow through a lone soldier, wood-chopper, or bullwhacker.

Hunton had built a log house on La Prele Creek about four miles from the fort, as well as a blacksmith shop and a charcoal pit. He was engaged not only in hauling freight, but in supplying the fort with wood. A number of us bullwhackers and some ex-soldiers did chopping for him at the rate of $4.00 a cord. The contract was practically filled, and most of the men had returned to Hunton's camp, when one of the woodchoppers, Jesse Hammond, an elderly man, stayed out alone in the hills too long. The result was that he never did return. When he was found, his body was literally filled with arrows. The friends of Jesse naturally were furious over this murderous work. Soldiers and bullwhackers forgot their feud, for the time, to turn their energies toward the exterminating of their common lurking foe.

"Stretched beside the trail, he lay dying."

CHAPTER EIGHT

SCOOTER BILL'S MONUMENT

"Come on, you Tex; fill up that bow —
   Git out o' here; you're too dang slow!
Bin on this job all night — go 'long!" —
   This the tenor of the bullpuncher's song.

The sand was deep and the night was dark,
   Tho' Venus twinkled like a spark,
When out the blackness there came a yell;
   From a Sioux it was — a scream from hell.

The crack of his rifle, like snap of a whip,
   Caused Scooter Bill's bulls to double their clip.
They filled their bows and pawed the sands,
   On the road to the Hills thro' the great Bad Lands.

But what stirred the team to increase its gait
   Left Scooter Bill in a helpless state —
Dead, to be exact, beside the desert road;
   The team plowed on without Bill's goad.

They buried Bill, his pals did, where he fell,
    And of this weird thing my story will tell.
Sufficient to say, tho', in this bit of rhyme,
    His tomb is of gold and will last for all time.

The chuck of the wheels on an iron axle was all that broke the stillness of the night, except, of course, the swishing of the tails of the horned beasts of burden. Seven yoke of oxen bent against their yokes of pinion, when suddenly out of the darkness, mingled with a yell, came the crack of a rifle.

Oxen, straining, bent even deeper into the bows about their necks, for, truth to tell, the crack from the rifle was only an imitation of the customary report from the business end of the bullwhacker's long lash — a sound that meant to the oxen, "Get out o' here!"

But the Sioux bullet had silenced the whip and the voice of its manipulator, for back there a few yards, stretched in the cactus beside the trail, he lay dying. Upon his ashen face there was a tiny crimson line representing the fast-ebbing life within the clay known to denizens of the Bad Lands as "Scooter Bill."

On plowed the team of seven yoke of oxen, for there were other intermittent cracks of the Sioux "whip," which had apparently taken up the task surrendered by Scooter Bill, until finally they came to deeper sand. There, the rifle-whip having ceased, they stood stock still, until, one by one as was their wont when allowed to stop, they rested on their bellies.

But back there a few rods was a gathering of men come up from the trailing units of the wagon train — grim-visaged and determined plainsmen, every one. And the picture is in this colloquy:

"Dave, you be sworn."

"Yes, sir; gimme the oath."

"You, Dave Springer, do you solemnly swear on your word of honor that you will kill on sight, wherever you meet him, any full blood of the Sioux, Cheyenne, or Arapahœ tribe?"

"I do."

And so the oath was taken by twenty hardy frontiersmen as it was administered by Neill Watson, wagon boss, as they waited for the return of the scouting party that had gone to circle the vicinity.

Spoke Watson:

"Get the shovels from the mess wagon; some one rip out a tailgate — one board, anyway; and some one — you, Jim, I guess — you can write, can't ye? You put Bill's name on the board. Damn them Injuns! Say, you, Sam, help Joe roll that new two-year-ol' robe o' mine around Bill, and take off his ca'tridge belt.

"That's right; now lower him in — easy, boys, easy — and put this piece of buckskin over his face, Joe, to keep the sand out of his eyes and mouth. Damn them Injuns! Not a stone anywhere around to cover this grave. The wolves won't have to dig a bit to get him, 'cause the wind will soon shift this sand; but we'll do our best to mark this spot — Damn them Injuns!"

Just after the burial had taken place, Ed Brown rode in on his herd pony and dismounted. The day was breaking. Every face as it looked toward Ed contained an inquiry, which he answered before any one spoke:

"Yes, I got one o' 'em; here's his left ear. But what d'ye think them Injuns left in their camp over yonder? This —" And Ed Brown produced a piece of quartz. "This," he continued, "is a sample of a gunny sackful.

Lazy devils never mined it, of course — stole it from some one trailing out o' the hills to a smelter."

"Fine," said Watson, "fine; just what we want. Open up the grave, Joe; scrape off a few shovelsful, and we'll go get that quartz."

Twenty-six years later, when a surveying crew for a railroad came upon the pyramid of quartz, there was no headbcard to indicate that Scooter Bill was buried there or that it was any one's grave. They were puzzled, for it looked like the corner-post job of some early-day government surveyor; perhaps it was a cairn left by General Dodge's first crew under Samuels, who had run a line a hundred miles north of the one finally chosen for the U. P., the discoverers surmised.

So these later-day surveyors proceeded to remove the pieces of rock forming the cairn, and found the quartz had been cemented together; but they broke the pieces apart, and in the center, just above the clean white bones of the bullwhacker, they found a tin can, which once had contained either corn or tomatoes. In the can was a slip of paper telling the story of Scooter Bill's tragic end, and adding that his pals, on the way back from Two-Bit Gulch, had reënforced the tomb with a lime-like substance called by geologists "formation," found in the vicinity of the Yellowstone geysers and the hot springs in the Black Hills.

Unless some vandal has disturbed the reconstructed cairn, it remains today, a reminder of the perils of navigation that beset the pilots of the prairie schooners of the seventies, not far from Alliance, Nebraska, in what is now known as Box Butte County.

The quartz for Bill's tombstone came, no doubt, from the famous Homestake Mine on Deadwood Creek. If so, and it weighs a hundred pounds, it is a valuable tombstone, for some of the first samples that went to smelters at Denver and Omaha from the mine were worth $6000 a ton.

"The Buckskin finally cut off a lone Indian who had
dismounted to drink from a spring."

CHAPTER NINE

THE BUCKSKIN MILITIA

IT WAS a succession of such tragedies as the killing of
Jesse Hammond and that depicted in the story of
Scooter Bill which brought about the Buckskin Militia.
Things got so warm one spring in the vicinity of Fort
Fetterman that the thirty or forty citizens camping
outside the military reservation organized a secret
society known by that name. The determination was to
avenge the deaths of Jesse Hammond and of others
whom Sioux arrows had killed.

The only qualification for membership in the Buckskins was a willingness to take the oath, which was as
follows:

"I, John Smith, do solemnly swear that I will shoot
on sight any male Indian, no matter whether he is
attacking me or other white men, stealing or attempting
to steal my property or the property of others, or whether
he is approaching or moving from me. Furthermore, I

will answer any call from another member of this band, or any other good white citizen, for assistance in the destruction of any male Indian found on the south side of the North Platte River; and will join in any raid upon an Indian camp when called upon by the Chief Buckskin. So help me God."

This oath was taken while standing on the stump of a cottonwood tree in the La Prele bottoms, the candidate being loaded down with as many log chains as he could hold; and the ceremony, usually held on a moonlight night, was as weird a sight as one can imagine.

The raids from the north continued nearly all summer. Several more white men were killed — one a lone prospector who thought there was mineral in the hills southwest of Fort Fetterman and near old Fort Caspar.

One of the Buckskins, hunting antelope one day in the vicinity of La Bonte Creek, crossed the trail of a single tepee, or family, and three ponies. This he knew from the lodgepole tracks made by a cayuse dragging the poles over the ground. The Buckskin took the trail, keeping well out of sight, but finally cut off a lone Indian who had dismounted to drink from a spring, allowing his young buck sons to go on. Buckskin whistled to give his quarry the chance he would give a mad dog — and no more. Then he put a bullet in his head.

He remained on the spot from which he fired, waiting to hear from the rest of the tepee, which he did in a few minutes, although the young bucks kept out of sight. They fired a few shots before Buckskin decided to make a dash, and when he did, it was a race of ten miles to a ford in the Platte. The young bucks escaped. Buckskin returned to his "good Indian," removed a lock of his hair, and took his gun and ammunition and a greasy card from the folds of his blanket, upon which some white man had written:

> This is Cut Nose, a "Good"
> Sioux Indian; but he is a
> Murderer and Thief.

There was a big session of the Buckskin Militia a few nights later, and great rejoicing. Cut Nose was a whole tribe of Indians in himself, and many dark crimes had been laid at his door by the white men who were engaged in freighting food to the Indian agencies and army posts.

It must be understood that there were no settlers or settlements or families in this section of Wyoming at this time; therefore there were never any of those horrible affairs common farther East a hundred years or more ago. There were no women and children for these Indians to kill, and year in and year out the fight was between them and bullwhackers, a few ranchmen, — not more than half a dozen, — government woodchoppers, and a few prospectors.

The professional hunters usually "stood in" with the red men, being possessed of some kind of magic that was never fully explained. In those days beaver, bear, buffalo, deer, antelope, and other game abounded. The hunter was likely to have a hut or "dugout" near a beaver dam; and it usually was well supplied with food, and sometimes a squaw was the hunter's companion. Her relatives were sure of good treatment, and I presume for that reason the relatives were able to give the "squaw man" protection. Still, hunters were murdered, but not often.

Finally, along in July, after the grass had lost its sap and turned brown, one of the Buckskins saddled up his pinto horse one day, strapped a blanket, a pone of bread, and a piece of bacon to his saddle, and giving free play to his Rowell spur, waved his hat and yelled as he dashed away:

"Goodby, boys; see you again in a few days. I'm goin' to put an end to these raids."

His brother Buckskins thought he was crazy — some of them did. But one or two winked and looked wise; and about sixty hours later, when some of the "Militia" had almost forgotten him, Buckskin rode up, unsaddled his pinto, punched him in the ribs, and said, "There now, old boy, go up the creek and enjoy yourself. Eat yourself to death, and I'll know where to find you when I want you. No Indian will get you."

When the boys crowded around him, he vouchsafed this much information:

"From a point twenty miles east of this spot to a spot twenty miles west of Fort Laramie, — on the north side of the Platte, — as far as the eye can reach in a northerly direction, and you know that's considerable distance, there is just one charred mass — every blade of grass has been burned."

There was no more trouble that season — no feed for the Indian ponies within a hundred miles of the fort to the north of the river.

"Two of them wheeled quickly and started for me."

CHAPTER TEN

A FOOLHARDY BOY

MY own chance to carry the oath of the Buckskin Militia into effect came soon enough. As I think of the incident now, I marvel at some of the wild-eyed notions I had and some of the foqlish things I did as a youngster. I wonder that I am on earth with all my limbs, a responsible hold on my mind, and able to remember so vividly some of my experiences. One of these, when all the facts are known, sounds, in the telling, as though I must have lacked every particle of fear of death, whereas, as sure as I live, I was then very much afraid to die.

One day while at Hunton's station close to the Fort Fetterman military reservation line, the report was brought to us that a band of Sioux had crossed the Platte River at a ford a few miles east of Fort Fetterman, and that it would be wise policy to fetch cattle and horses from their feeding grounds a mile or two up La Prele closer to the log house and blacksmith shop.

This was done. However, previous to the receipt of this report, I had planned to go into the fort on some errand; so I mounted my pony and started.

"If you see any Injun on the way in," shouted Ed Smith, Hunton's blacksmith-bullwhacker, "don't forget your oath," and I replied that I wouldn't.

I hadn't the slightest notion in the world that I was to see an Indian; so when a mile from the cabin I saw riding along a ridge east of the creek a blanketed form, his pony walking slowly, I got into the bushes as quickly as my pony could carry me. From the maneuvers of the figure on the hill, I was sure he had not seen me. His pony's head was lowered and he was making very slow progress, while his rider was humped up in his blanket.

Dismounting, I knelt on the ground in a little opening, took deliberate aim, and fired. I believed that the mark was well within range, but it wasn't; my shot kicked up the gravel at least ten yards short. But what a change there was in the appearance of that outfit on the hill! The pony developed into a "high school class" prize winner in a horse show, rearing and plunging and rapidly carrying his rider from me, while the latter had quickly slid from a crouching, sleeping-like position to one hanging on the off side from me, only a toe or two being in sight; but I arose and blazed away again, well knowing that I couldn't hit the mark.

I hurried on to Fort Fetterman and told Post Trader Tillotson what I had done. He was sure I had shot at a white man, and laughed at me. But he told me the commander at the fort had received word that two bands of Sioux had crossed the river, and one of them was somewhere near old Fort Caspar, now the city of Caspar. Some scouts had started out in the direction of

"I knelt on the ground, took deliberate aim, and fired."

the ford to the east, however, believing there was more likelihood of finding their trail there than to the west of Fetterman, where there was no fording place.

Soon afterward I started back to Hunton's camp. A half mile or so from the fort I decided to turn to the west on the old Oregon Trail and see what I could find in the way of Indian signs — about the most foolish thing a foolish boy could do. But I was now at least eighteen, man's size, and had begun to grow a beard, which, added to hair at least a foot long, hanging down my back, made a mighty attractive possession in the way of a scalplock for Indians who made it their special business to collect such things. I seemed, as it now appears, ready and willing to contribute mine, although, as I remember fifty years afterward, I had no such notion at all. But I was curious, and that is the only way I can explain my action in leaving the creek bottom and deliberately hunting, single-handed, for a band of Indians who were on the warpath.

I soon saw where tepee poles had been dragged along the ground, and I mounted a high hill, looking in every direction. There wasn't a living thing in sight, but I kept going, every step my horse took carrying me farther away from the fort and the men at Hunton's.

Finally, not a half mile ahead of me, I spied about twenty mounted Indians. They saw me at the same time, and two of them wheeled quickly and started for me. My old pony was slow always, and it was necessary when I wanted him to go faster than a walk to rub the spurs on his ribs and ply the quirt vigorously: and even then he had no speed. I jabbed him frightfully and lashed him with all the strength I had, but that wasn't what made him turn into a "Jay-Eye-See" or a "Goldsmith Maid," a "Maud S," or a "Harvester." He developed both the trotting and running gaits of those famous old-time racers; he racked, he tried to lope, he ran as they used to run at Sheepshead Bay or Churchill Downs, because there rang in his ears something he understood and feared even more than I did. It was a hair-raising sound he had heard many a time before; while this was my first experience.

How those warriors did yell! And how my cayuse did leap, lope, bound, and carry me back to La Prele Creek, too close to the fort for the comfort of the Sioux.

I was soon safe, — sooner than it has taken me to write it, — but I had had all I wanted of trailing Indians on my own account. After watering Dexter — for I called him that thereafter — I went slowly home to Hunton's, to have another surprise. As soon as I entered the log house I saw lying on the hard earth floor a very dark-visaged, black-haired man, writhing, and, as I at first thought, dying.

It was Seminole, whom I had seen on my first day as a bullwhacker near Cheyenne. He had come to the camp, the boys said, laughing fit to kill, telling them that I had taken a couple of shots at him. They plied him with liquor, and up to a few minutes before my arrival, when he became speechless, he had been crying in several languages, "I'm a dying calf! I'm a dying calf!"

Before night he was sober enough to talk straight, and he spoke very good English. He pretended to have a score to settle with me, and dared me to go outside and shoot at a hundred yards with our rifles; but when I showed a disposition to do it, he began to laugh, put his arm around my neck, and, in a half-drunken manner, said, "Forgiveness, forgiveness; fool boy, fool boy."

That was the last I ever saw of Seminole, the desperado. A few years ago I learned that the misguided man had finally paid the penalty for murder with his life at Cheyenne, where he was legally executed.

"I saw climbing down the bluff a half-dozen young bucks."

CHAPTER ELEVEN

A BRUSH WITH YOUNG BRAVES

A YEAR or so after my race to save my scalp I had another bit of excitement with a band of young braves.

On one trip to Red Cloud Agency, on White Clay River up in the northwest corner of Nebraska, it fell to my lot late one hot summer afternoon to fill the water kegs at a swift-running creek which was, no doubt, a tributary of the river. We were to make a dry camp a few miles ahead, perhaps a day's drive from the agency, and the bulls were to be driven back to the creek for the night. The water for drinking and cooking had to be hauled. Another man was detailed to help. While our bulls, tired from the hard drive of the day, lay down in their tracks on the trail, we began to fill several kegs. The water was dipped up with quart cups and poured through auger holes, which we corked when the kegs were filled. While we were engaged at this slow work,

68

the rest of the train moved on slowly, and soon the last wagon was out of sight. Then my partner, hearing something moving in the brush, arose, saying, "I heard something; maybe it's Injuns."

We looked around and saw nothing, but the leaders of my team jumped up and stretched, and then more of the bulls got up and looked into the bushes. I dropped my cup and reached for my gun.

My partner ran to his team, which had also risen and started to twist around to one side of his wagons. They seemed worried, and I began to be uneasy. I knew there was something unusual going on, but I could neither hear nor see anything either on the sunburned bluffs of the creek or in the green bottoms.

I waded out and looked upstream and downstream. Seeing nothing out of the ordinary, I resumed my bailing of the clear, cool water into a keg. Then suddenly I heard a rattling of gravel, and in a second I saw climbing down the bluff a half-dozen young bucks, not one of whom was more than fourteen years old. They wore only breechclouts, carried bows and arrows, and one of them had a spear, whose metal point, as I distinctly remember, shone brightly in the sun. Their copper skins also glistened, for they were greasy, and their hair hung in braids like those of little girls.

My gun was in my hands in a jiffy, but I did not point it. I stood erect and faced the young warriors — and they were all of that; for be it known that the best fighters of the tribes that lived in that country at the time were the very young boys, who would not be controlled by older and sometimes more peaceful Indians. Many an unfortunate massacre has been traced to the eagerness of Indian boys to shine as braves.

Though our cargo consisted of bacon, sugar, and other

provisions, being freighted out there into the wilds to feed these very same youngsters, yet I admit I was scared and sure of trouble. There was but one way out of it, I decided, and that was to appear not to be afraid; so I smiled as the first young buck approached me, saying something and pointing to the wagon. Of course I couldn't understand, and made no hostile move or sound until they swarmed upon one of the wagons and began to investigate the contents of my jockey box and tear open a large gunny sack containing brown sugar. Then I approached with gun aimed and ordered them off, still smiling.

They demurred, and one of the young devils bent his bow and fixed an arrow which was pointed directly at me. I pointed the gun at his head and he laughed. The others climbed down, and then my partner came from behind the wagons with his gun also in position for action. He had straightened out the cattle, which at first seemed ready to stampede to the rear and perhaps break off a tongue or overturn the wagons. He did a good job, and was less worried about the intentions of our visitors than I was. We decided to take no chances, however, and to hold the upper hand, which we plainly saw we were playing. So I put the gun in the face of one of the youngsters, pointed to an army cup and marched him to the spring, where he very docilely helped fill the rest of the kegs, being assisted by the others. Then I took a cup, filled it with the brown sugar, and divided it among them. When we strung out our teams, we marched the six would-be warriors to camp with us.

I admit I enjoyed the praise given us for our determination not to be bluffed and robbed by the young Indians. Mr. Clay said that if we had shown the least sign of fear or weakness, they would have taken everything we had, looted our jockey boxes, and decamped, and perhaps killed us. As it was, Clay, keeping the young bucks with us and feeding them until we reached the warehouses, turned them over to the agency authorities.

"Suddenly there was a swish. It was an arrow!"

CHAPTER TWELVE

GUARDING THE OX TRAIN

OUR adventures with the Indians were not generally of the tragic sort; but we had always to be on the watch to keep clear of trouble. And frequently we did get close to a real fight with the redskins.

At one time, after the brush with the young bucks, I was assigned by the wagon boss, Watson, to mount a "pinto" pony and ride all day at least one thousand yards away from the trail and keep to the high places where I could see what, if anything, was going on in the vicinity. He had instructed me to dismount and examine any signs of life on the ground where it was bare, or in the grass. When I found such signs, I was to fire one shot from my revolver to let the bullwhackers know that they had "company" not far off. My orders were, if I saw one Indian or a hundred, to shoot, not once, but three times in rapid succession, and then gallop to the wagon trail with details.

The movement across the desert-like country this day began at four in the morning and continued until after dark. I was well equipped with an army Springfield of large caliber, forty rounds in my belt, two Remington revolvers, and a butcher knife with a five-inch blade for the possibility of close quarters. I had a bottle of spring water and a saddlebag full of sandwiches of bread and fried bacon, and plenty of tobacco.

Perhaps you imagine I was thinking of my soft bed at home or a shot from ambush that would leave my skeleton bleaching in a sandy desert sun after it had been stripped of its flesh by wolves; or that I wished some one else had been chosen to guard one side of the overland train of flour, bacon, corn, and sugar, and its custodians; but my thoughts were not these. It was one of the proudest days of my life, and I know I shall never forget it. I had been highly honored by Watson, and I appreciated it.

I never dreamed of death when I got my orders, because I was young and foolish. Sometimes it is called bravery, but that is not the right word. It cannot be described, unless it is called blind or reckless indifference. Perhaps that isn't it. Anyway, as I mounted and galloped away and waited on a neighboring knoll for the outfit to string out along the sandy trail, I really hoped I shouldn't be disappointed. I wanted an eventful day and fairly prayed for it. "I hope," I ruminated to myself half aloud, "that I cross a tepee trail, at least, even if I don't get my eye on an Indian."

It wasn't long until I began to wonder, for it was still barely daylight, if it wouldn't be possible for a buck of good aim to pick me off, especially if the buck practiced the usual tactics of concealing himself behind a sand dune or a butte. For this reason I kept my pony moving, reasoning that it is harder to hit a moving target than one which is stationary.

My pony appeared to be a dead one, even when a spur was roughly rubbed upon his belly. Suddenly, however, when the train had got well out of camp and the teams strung along for a mile, he began to prick up his ears. He had grown interested in something, for he insisted on frequent stops, moved his ears back and forth, and snorted lightly. Finally, it seemed next to impossible to get him to move. I felt certain the pony had been owned by Indians at some time and was of the trick variety, being trained to a brand of treachery that meant he might dash with me straight into a band of redskins.

While these things were passing through my brain, my only concern was that the train was leaving me and that I was not guarding it. I heard a coyote's mournful note, but that was a common occurrence, although I wondered if it couldn't be possible that an Indian was doing the howling. It sounded like an imitation.

The pony snorted some more but stood still. Finding my blunt-pointed spurs were not getting me anywhere, I unsheathed my butcher knife and pricked my cayuse on the back. He tried to buck, but he wore a double cinch — one fore and one aft — and it kept him on all fours.

Things were getting worse. The voices of the bullwhackers, yelling at their teams, grew fainter and fainter as the outfit slowly but surely put distance between my companions and me. Then suddenly there was a sound that resembled the dropping of a stick in the water, preceded by a distinct swish, as if it had been thrown through the air like a boomerang.

Then the pinto got busy. It was an arrow!

There were several more. One of them clipped the pommel of the saddle before I thought of my orders to fire — once, on sight of disturbed grass or a moccasin track on bare ground; three times, upon sighting an Indian.

I let go with my Springfield in the supposed direction of the enemy and headed for the trail, which I readily found. In a short time I had caught up with the mess wagon. This always made the rear guard of the train. The night herder was inside and the extra herd horses were tied behind.

Watson, galloping toward the rear, met me there.

"What is it, boy?" he shouted.

"They got a piece of my Texas pommel," I replied, "but I don't know where the arrow came from. I'll go back and see."

I had wheeled my pony to strike back to take up my station a thousand yards from the trail, when Watson said laughingly:

"You're crazy. Wait a minute till I send word up ahead to corral."

"You" — to the mess-wagon driver — "untie them hosses, saddle 'em up, and wait for Blucher Brown and Archer; they'll be back in a minute."

As the sun peeped over a rise in the land, I waited impatiently. So did the pony, for the miserable Indian-bred cuss had a nose that was keen to the smoky smell of an Indian or to the odor of other horses, especially of his own breed. He was all animation and ready to go.

When the party finally got away, Watson, turning to me as we galloped side by side along the high spots near the back trail, said:

"If yer not afraid, pull out ahead with that pony and lead the way."

I pressed the Rowell spur to the pony's side. He responded like a real cow-pony, much to my surprise, and before Watson could gather his breath to call me back, I led them by two hundred yards. Finally he did manage to yell through his laughter:

"Hold on, you danged idiot! I didn't mean —"

But he didn't finish the sentence, although he continued yelling, this time expressing himself to the effect:

"My hoss has been creased in the neck! Dismount, give me your hoss and lead mine back to the outfit; we'll take care of these galoots!"

I protested, but it was no use, and returned. When I joined the whackers, they had corralled and gathered the bulls inside the wagons, which formed two half circles on a high spot near the trail. There were several other horses in the outfit; so I quickly slipped the boss's fine saddle on the back of a buckskin of the cow-puncher variety and sped back to the scene of action.

But it was all over. The sun was too high for further ambushing; so the Indians disappeared, skulking at safe distance to wait for darkness and perhaps other prey. The only evidence of their presence was a spot of crumpled grass behind a knoll where several of them had lain in complete safety while they tried to send me to the Happy Hunting Grounds.

After another shift of mounts and saddles and bridles, I again took my post one thousand yards from the trail and rode along, smoking my pipe and munching sandwiches and drinking the spring water.

At ten o'clock camp was struck for the midday stop. A creek of sweet cold water ran by our noon camping place through some small hills covered with stunted pines. A few miles away was a range of black mountains, beyond the Bad Lands and sand.

It was here that I was promoted to the position of assistant wagon boss and presented with a big sorrel horse called "America" (because he was not Indian-bred). Watson gave me the lead team to drive in the outfit. This meant that, in coöperation with the "big boss," I should help select the camps, govern the speed of the "train," look after the manifests, act as check clerk in loading and unloading, and besides wear a red sash to designate my official position.

I took my honors modestly. I was surprised, in fact, and couldn't understand it until some one told me the "old man" was pleased when I took the wounded horse back to the train, saddled up another, and returned to help find where the arrows came from.

"A big buck stood silently for a full minute, listening."

CHAPTER THIRTEEN

RATTLESNAKES AND REDSKINS

THE night herder's song waked me at four in the morning — the first streak of day — and I didn't have time to pull on my boots before the bulls were inside the corral; so, in bare feet, I yoked my fourteen head and then proceeded to pull on the cowhides, roll up my blankets, and throw them on my trail wagon. Due to the haste — for nearly every one else in the outfit was ready to "pull out" in response to the wagon boss's order — I proceeded to pull on the left boot without the usual precautions. My fingers were in the straps as I sat on the ground, and in another minute my toes would have been in the boot. But the rattler that had spent the night in it stuck out his head. I shook him out, first calling my pard to come with his whip.

After the rattler was dead I plucked off eleven beautifully graduated white rattles and a black button, later on adding them to a hatband of several hundred which

I had sewed together, using silk thread and a cambric needle. The other boot was tenantless.

The blankets, in a neat roll secured by a heavy leather strap, were thrown on top of the freight in the trailer, and away we went for a dry camp in the Bad Lands, where we spent six hours of the middle of the day hiding under our wagons to escape the hot rays of the sun.

A late afternoon start ended at nine in a moonlit camp on a creek that ran swiftly through chalk-like bluffs — perhaps the head-waters of the Niobrara River. In those days none but a geographer or a government surveyor knew the names of many of the waterways, if they had names. It had been a hard drive through deep sand most of the way, and after the bulls had been relieved of their yokes and the chains that held the teams together, all hands raced for the water, both for internal and external purposes.

Our night camp was on a flat between the bluffs and a few yards from the stream in a most inviting spot, the edge of the crooked channel being lined with stunted and gnarled box-elder, while farther back were a few dozen dead and gaunt cottonwoods. Some small bushes grew in clumps here and there, but our camp commanded a good view, even in the night, of the country for a mile in at least two directions — north and south.

Though I was tired, it was too brilliant a night even in this wilderness to go to bed; for a youngster who had acquired two revolvers, a Winchester rifle, and a butcher knife believed the crumpled grass he had seen at the edge of the creek indicated the presence not far away of others of the human family, and he intended to find out about it. He had confided this suspicion to one other youth of the outfit, and as the supper campfire died down to a bed of coals and a cool wind began to fan the hot earth these boys stole out of camp, waded the creek, and carefully examined the earth up and down its margin until they came upon a distinct moccasin, pony, and lodgepole trail. They followed it along the bottoms for two miles to a jutting bluff, where around the corner they saw six tepees, near which were picketed several ponies.

All was silent as the boys, concealed in a safe spot, viewed the scene. Then there was a sound, low at first, like the crooning of a mother to a babe, which grew louder and louder, until finally there emerged from one of the tepees a big buck who stood silently for a full minute, listening. He wore nothing but a breechclout, and over his shoulder hung a buckskin strap upon which were attached the arrows for the big bow held in his hand. He did wear a bonnet, which consisted principally of feathers that looked exactly like some of the creations worn by women of the present day.

When he had located the sound he moved toward the hiding boys, but stopped at the nearest tepee. The crooning grew to a lamentation. Then other tepees showed signs of life, and in a few moments bucks, squaws, and papooses were running hither and thither in a bewildering way. But the boys remained silent, for there was no sign of a movement of camp and not an indication that there was an outside alarm. Then what could it be? What was all this fuss about? The lamentations became louder and louder and the excitement apparently greater.

Finally a number of squaws who had gone to the creek bottom appeared in the center of the little camp. They carried bundles of green willows, dozens of large hard-head boulders, and rawhide receptacles filled with water; also a bundle of dry fagots.

After the stones had been piled in a neat heap a fire was built upon them which was allowed to burn briskly for half an hour. Then the coals and ashes were brushed off and a tent-like covering put over a quickly woven basket-like structure that had been built over the stones. Then the water was dashed upon the stones and the steam began to ascend.

Presently out from a tepee came a squaw with a bundle which she gently shoved under the skin-covered caldron of steam.

"Say," said one of the boys, "are you on?"

"Sure enough," the other whispered; "they are giving that kid a Turkish bath."

And that's what they were doing; but it wasn't Turkish — just Injun.

Returning to camp the boys proceeded to slip into their blankets quietly and go to sleep, saying nothing about what they had seen. They believed the straggling band of Arapahoes were not on the war-path and had work for the "medicine man" — the big buck they first saw come out of his tepee.

You have no idea how cautiously the boys went about getting the blankets off the wagon so as not to disturb the boss, a man they feared. So they moved noiselessly.

One threw his roll of blankets from the top of the trailer and the other caught the bundle and proceeded to flatten it out into a comfortable bed when he heard a familiar noise, and forgetting that they were to be silent, the youth on the ground yelled:

"Look out — a rattler!"

It woke up the whole camp. The snake had occupied

the blankets from four that afternoon, at least, until this time — midnight. Perhaps he had slept with the boy until four in the morning. I think he did; anyway, he had rolled him up and put him where found.

"Crawling . . . to Pinto . . . in the coulee." (See page 165.)

CHAPTER FOURTEEN

THE CIVILIZATION OF PIPESTONE

WHEN Pipestone was a boy his father was an agency Indian, a member of a blanket tribe, and a recipient of flour, bacon, sugar, and tobacco from his Uncle Sam, that was doled out at stated periods at Red Cloud Agency on White River. At fifteen, he rode a pony of his own, was the possessor of a Sharps rifle, a scalping knife, a breechclout, a pair of moccasins, and a leather belt once worn by a soldier in the Regular Army. But Pipestone, who was then called Ten, had seldom had any ammunition for his Sharps; therefore on his forays about the country surrounding the agency, sometimes as far away as the Niobrara and the North Platte, he carried his bow and arrows.

Ten had several companions of his own age, one of whom, Glass Arrow, was a descendant of Chief Spotted Tail, and therefore himself to some extent recognized as a chieftain by his youthful marauders; for they were marauders of the very worst kind — much worse, in fact, than the older Indians, who had begun to realize how futile it was to oppose the orders of the white man's government to stay in a certain restricted territory. They were, in truth, a band of young murderers, and made more trouble for the white bullwhacker and mule-skinner who freighted in the then almost uninhabited country than all the old bucks of the Sioux, Cheyenne, or Arapahoe tribes.

The thing these young Indians most sought was powder and shells — cartridges for their obsolete guns that had come to them largely through trade from older Indians, who understood that a Sharps rifle was about as useless for marauding or hunting purposes as would be a saddle and no horse, though they had no use for a saddle unless it was one of the pack variety for the transportation of game.

The only time that Ten could be found at Red Cloud or Pine Ridge was on those days when the government representative and his assistant were apportioning the flour, bacon, and an occasional steer to the heads of the tepees gathered at the agency. The rest of his time was spent, with his companions, in attempting to collect ammunition from passing wagon trains either through honorable barter or raid; but they never found any Sharps ammunition, or any other kind that would fit their out-of-date guns, though they did find plenty of powder in the more modern Springfield cartridges which they tried to use in discarded shells without success.

Sometimes Glass Arrow and Ten, who were leaders of the various expeditions, swarmed down upon a bull-whackers' camp in friendly fashion, entering the corral slowly and with no whooping or other demonstration that was not entirely peaceful. Then, while Ten and

Glass Arrow sought out the wagon boss, and by signs and almost unintelligible guttural sounds indicated what was wanted, the others scattered over the camp to pick up anything portable they could lay their hands on while the white men's eyes were cleverly drawn elsewhere by some unusual maneuver or prank of another young buck. Sometimes they got ammunition in this way, frequently a chisel, a butcher knife, or a belt.

But if unsuccessful, they retired at a signal from one of the leaders, and when at a safe distance fired a few arrows at the white men, a sort of goodby salute. This usually meant the saddling of the night-herd horses and a chase, though never very far or into any place where the whites could be surrounded by a possible band that had remained in the background. Usually Ten and his gang got away safely, for they nearly always had good ponies and a start that was safe and sure before they fired their salute.

On one occasion, however, Ten and Glass Arrow made a miscalculation in this way:

They had entered the Clay corral and stolen a couple of knives and a beltful of cartridges, but were discovered in the act of pilfering the last belt; whereupon Charley Clay, owner of the outfit, and his wagon boss, John Lord, mounted their saddleless herd horses, and were ready for the chase before the youngsters left the corral. The young bucks broke away, however, in a concerted dash, in two parties of eight each, and when they reached a point a hundred yards down the road, sent their arrows whizzing back at Clay and Lord, who stopped and, taking deliberate aim, fired. Ten dropped his bow, wavered a moment, slid to the off side of his pony, and apparently was about to fall into the sagebrush beside the road when there came a yell from down the trail, followed by several shots from a pistol which was in the hands of Luke Miller, a bullwhacker belonging to the outfit who had the night before left camp and ridden forty-one miles to Fort Laramie to play faro bank for one hour. Luke was returning, and he arrived just in time to meet one of the bands of eight, led by Ten, as it surmounted a small rise in the trail. This broke up Ten's party, and they scattered in every direction. By this time several other herd horses had been saddled by men in camp and the hunt was on.

Dave Borden and William Frank saw Ten slipping as he sped over the rolling fields of sage, and believed they could capture him alive; so they chose him as their objective, and there was a race that would, if filmed at this late day, make a thriller that would turn the head of any boy and cause his elders to hold their breath. Borden and Frank, both of whom were good shots, never stopped firing their Springfields, but they aimed not to kill either Ten or his horse; they knew he was wounded, and they wanted to get him and deliver him to Agent McGillicuddy at the agency, if possible, thus complying with the request of the government's representatives that they kill only when absolutely necessary. Finally Ten's pony stumbled, as most Indian ponies do, and Ten slipped off, sat down, and waited for Borden and Frank to come up. Ten's left arm had been broken by Clay's shot and hung loosely by his side. But he smiled, said something in Sioux, and stretched out on his back. The pony, out of wind, assumed the posture of the regulation Indian cayuse, spreading out his legs and lowering his head almost to the ground, apparently wholly winded and indifferent to anything going on around him.

Frank had an extra bandanna, which he wound into

"Pipestone . . . shaded his eyes as he faced the burning sun."
(See page 165.)

a rope and tied around Ten's bleeding arm. Then the boys lifted him to his pony's back and all three jogged slowly back to camp beside Clear Creek near its junction with the Chugwater. At camp they met the rest of the men, who had given short chase to the others of the band without result, and it was soon decided to wash and dress Ten's wound with a mild solution of Mustang liniment, a remedy always used by the bullwhackers for wounds of man and beast. It usually stopped the flow of blood and healed a wound quickly.

Ten was indifferent and sullen, and made no sound — not even a whimper about his wound; neither did he object to being loaded into a big Bain wagon and tied to the tailgate. It was a two-day drive to Fort Laramie, where it was at first proposed to turn Ten over to the army authorities; but later on Clay determined not to let the commandant know he had an Indian prisoner, preferring to deliver him to McGillicuddy, though the capture had been made south of the Platte, where the military authorities were in control of all such things.

After the party left the fort, a sharp lookout was kept for the rest of the young bucks, in anticipation of a raid, especially in the early morning hours in the vicinity of the Rawhide Buttes. It was well that this precaution was taken, for on the third morning out from the fort, in what was now the Indians' own country, unmistakable signs of the presence of the young band were noted, — moccasin tracks, the tracks of unshod ponies, trampled grass, and the like. But no attempt was made to shoot into the train while in camp or on the move until the lead team entered a little valley between two large buttes in the bottom of a dry creek bed. Then there was a shower of arrows. None of them did any damage to the drivers, who kept right on as if nothing unusual were happening, until every one of the thirty teams had emerged on a table of cactus at the north end of the valley or coulee. Then the wagon boss ordered the outfit corralled, and the eight horses in the outfit were hastily saddled and eight bullwhackers were soon making the dirt fly on the back trail to a point where the high land could be reached in the open and beyond the fire of the young bucks.

When within two thousand yards of the covering where the bucks were supposed to be concealed, Clay, who led the party, dismounted, shouldered his rifle, and told Frank to stay with the horses while the others went the rest of the way afoot.

Clay knew there was but one point from which the young bucks could get off the spot, and that spot was now covered by eight bullwhackers. If the bucks determined to make a fight, it was going to be a siege. If they realized they were surrounded, they would either have to jump off a high bluff or run the gantlet, for there was neither water nor food in this desert spot, and Clay had determined to hold the fort at all hazards. All this time the Indians were slowly wending their way toward the bullwhackers, never dreaming that they were to be attacked; for when the wagon train left the little valley it was completely out of their view, and they never for a moment suspected that they would have to fight to get down into the valley. The hillside was covered with rocks and sage, so that there was no difficulty in making a steady and safe advance almost all the time under cover.

Soon a pony's head came around the corner, and in another instant a young buck was in full view. He saw nothing and came along without suspecting anything. In a minute more the second and third ponies and riders

were in view, when, at a signal from Clay, the seven
bullwhackers arose, within fifty yards of the bucks,
aimed their guns full at their heads, and demanded a
surrender. The buck in the lead attempted to bolt,
sticking his bare heels into the ribs of his pony to accel-
erate his speed. But a bullet from Clay's Winchester
pierced the pony's skull and he dropped to the ground.

Then the rest of the party emerged with hands raised
above their heads and were marched down the bluff to
the corralled outfit, Frank taking up the rear, while
Clay and his six companions remounted their herd
horses and surrounded the bucks, who sullenly passed
along as directed.

Not one of these Indian boys wore a stitch of clothing
except a breechclout and moccasins; their brown bodies
shone like silver as the hot sun beat down upon them,
and their ponies, lean from hard usage, were in a state
of collapse. In fact, they told Clay, through an interpreter who was met at Roaring Creek camp a few days
later, that they never would have surrendered if there
had been a single chance to escape from the bluff; but
the ponies were staggering, tough as they were, and they
couldn't rush the line that Clay and his companions had
formed.

Clay simply disarmed every one of the bucks and
allowed them to trail along, giving them a side of bacon,
a bag of wormy flour, and a chunk of beef for a little
camp they formed. However, before reaching White
River camp, where the water kegs were filled for a dry
camp that night on the plateau, Clay, by signs and
words that could be interpreted as kindly, motioned the
youngsters out of the corral. They were astonished, for
the interpreter had told them that they would no doubt
be sent to the dreaded Indian Territory, now Oklahoma,

if they were not indeed executed for their crimes. Ten, however, was still a cripple from his arm wound, a chip of the bone having been driven into the fleshy part of the arm and festered, giving him a great deal of pain, which he suffered heroically and in absolute silence. Consequently the kindly Clay decided to turn him over to the agency authorities, with the recommendation that he be advised that if ever caught again even visiting a bull-whackers' camp for the purpose of pilfering, he would be unceremoniously shot. He did this, and from that time on Ten and his pal, Glass Arrow, spent their young manhood in riding the trail between Red Cloud and the lower portion of the country set aside for the use of the Indians, calling themselves "policemen." These they really were by order of the agency authorities. They also acted as scouts and protectors for the bull outfits, turning away any strolling bands of marauding Indians who might have designs on the lives or property of the freighters.

Ten, now a man close to seventy years of age and known as "Pipestone," lives in a small cabin, built as a white man would build it, in a little coulee not far from Belle Fourche. He wears good clothes, talks the best of English and Canadian-French, and has a family of grown-up children who are also married and living at scattered points in the Black Hills. All have been educated in government schools, and are engaged in agricultural pursuits or other industries and live lives as fully civilized as any one. But none knows Pipestone as "Ten" except two or three ancient bullwhackers who survived the strenuous life of the early seventies and the subsequent storms and trials of life in various parts of these now thoroughly civilized United States.

Not long ago Pipestone listened to an old bullwhacker

recount the surrender at the big butte on the Cheyenne Trail. It took a half hour to tell it, and Pipestone was silent through it all to the end. Then he arose, and with all the dignity of an old chieftain he said, in a trembling voice, but earnestly:

"Friends, I was Ten, but I was young and foolish. I had listened for a year or more to the stories of my elders, — how they had been cheated and misused by the white man, and how they had killed and robbed the whites in revenge, but how, finally, my people had been backed up from pillar to post to the bad lands in the four corners of several great states. My young blood boiled, and with Glass Arrow — he died only five years ago — we organized a band to revenge the fathers and mothers and children who were now rounded up at an agency and prevented from going and coming in the country that was once so free to us all. But I little knew how foolish it was to try to oppose the march of education and civilization — mining, ranching, manufacturing. What did we know about it? Even the white man who came among us could not see what you see here in Douglas, down at Cheyenne, up at Hot Springs, over at Spearfish, and at Deadwood. We were simple children of the great plains, accustomed to our freedom and the hunt. We were carefree except when the soldiers came among us and told us that the Great Father had decided to move us yet a few hundred miles farther back, so that the white man could come in with his herds or his plow. Can you wonder that we resented it? And, friends, is it not wonderful that as a boy, a rover of the plains, with the spirit of the wolf, I should see, as I did when captured by the bullwhackers, that the fight was hopeless, and even more than that — foolish? The kindly treatment shown our little band those few days we were with them made the turn in my life, and I resolved, in face of the insults that I knew would be heaped upon me by members of my race, to be a good man. They called me as they did that eminent chief, Red Cloud, a squaw, but I lived through it, settled down with some thousands of others who saw the handwriting on the wall, went to the fine school the government provided, and here I am."

And then Pipestone rolled up the sleeve of a shirt that carried the trademark of a New Jersey factory and displayed the scar of the wound he had received so many years ago when he raided the bull outfit.

Today there isn't one band of wild Indians in America; the plains they roamed have been irrigated and are being farmed; the mountains where they hid are being drilled, bored, sluiced for precious metal; oil wells and refineries are within a few miles of the first meeting place of Clay and his bullwhackers and the band of youthful marauders.

To at least one of the whites who participated in many of these affairs, and who dodged the arrows of Pipestone's band, it is all very wonderful — but sad, after all; for while those were days of peril and hardship, they were exciting, and it is easy for him to place himself in Pipestone's boots and understand that even with all the benefits of civilization, still something that was delightful and fascinating about life has been squeezed out of it, never to return.

Snow had sealed the grass against the tough noses and even the hoofs of the hungry bulls.

CHAPTER FIFTEEN

BELATED GRACE FOR A CHRISTMAS DINNER

AFTER fighting through a ten-hour blizzard that swept across the plains from the Elk Mountain country, our wagon train reached the foothills of the Medicine Bow range, where there was shelter for the work cattle along a swift-running stream. The snow was piled in great drifts everywhere except upon exposed high spots, and it seemed impossible for us to proceed farther, for we knew that along the government trail just beyond, and one thousand feet higher, the drifts would be so deep that a long camp where we had stopped would be necessary.

Ten men were told off by the wagon boss to chop down young quaking-aspen trees, the bark and small twigs of which furnished appetizing fodder for the bulls. Another gang climbed a side hill and with axes felled a group of stunted pines for the side walls of a cabin; still others were sent into a "burnt and down" piece of

94

timber to gather well-seasoned dead pitch pine for firewood.

The storm lasted until six o'clock in the evening, and then continued as an old-fashioned heavy snowfall with no wind, increasing the level of the snow to the tops of the wheels of our corralled wagons. Apparently they were doomed to stay where they were until spring.

Next morning there was a let-up. Then the blizzard began again in all its fury — only such a blizzard as one can see in but one other place on earth, judging from Dana's description of his experience in going around the Horn. The cattle, with almost human intelligence, two hundred head of them, crowded toward the big bonfires of pitch, and with long faces looked mournfully upon the scene. They seemed to know, as we did, that the prospects were not bright for our caravan. Certainly there was no grass in sight now, not even on the round-topped knolls bordering our little valley, for the night fall of snow was heavy and damp, and finally, when the thermometer registered a few degrees below zero, the grass was sealed against the tough noses and even the hoofs of the hungry bulls. An attempt was made by a scouting party to find a clear feeding place on the back trail, but a day's investigation resulted in failure. Not a blade of grass could be found — all was sealed with a heavy crust that would, in most places, carry a horse and rider.

The storm continued, after an eight-hour let up, the temperature rising. Two feet more fell on top of the crust. Then came another blizzard and a new crust. After twenty-four hours still another blizzard came from the north, consisting of sleet and snow and some rain; it was like a sand storm in summer on the plains below. It was fierce, nearly freezing and blinding both men and cattle. The poor bulls were more forlorn than ever. They gnawed the very wood of the aspens, and there wasn't enough of that.

On the last crust of all this snow and sleet it was finally found possible to take the oxen farther along into the mountains, where four men drove them. Others went ahead with axes, and for two weeks cut aspens and sought out hidden protected places in the valleys where there were a few blades of grass and some succulent underbrush.

One day, when the sun was shining brightly on the white mantle and the distant peaks of the majestic mountains of blue stood out like a painting, Nath Williams, wagon boss, spoke:

"Do you know," he said to the fellows who were carving the carcass of a faithful old bullock, "that tomorrow is Christmas?" None had thought of it.

"And," he continued, "do you know we are liable to stay where we are until the Fourth of July, if we don't get a move on?" There were no suggestions.

"Furthermore," added Williams, "we haven't much else to eat but beef — there are just five 100-pound sacks of flour in the mess wagon — no bacon nor canned goods. It's a case of shoveling a road to Crane's Neck."

Crane's Neck was a mountain twist in the road, a mile from camp. If the road could be cleared to that point, there would be fair hauling for five miles in the range to another stretch that had been filled in places with from ten to twenty feet of snow, while one spot was covered by a slide from a mountain to a depth of forty feet and for a considerable distance along the trail.

For three hours plans were discussed, and it was finally determined to go to work with shovels and picks, but not until after Christmas. Our caravan included a blacksmith's forge and a regular wrecking outfit, and in a short time big wooden shovels were made from blocks of pine, with handles stoutly attached with iron bands.

The cook was a youth of twenty and had all the enthusiasm of the adventurer. He had spent a year on a whaler and knew what it meant to drift in the ice north of Point Barrow. This present situation, he said, was a picnic; so was the one in the Arctic. It couldn't be so bad that he wished to be snuggled away in a feather bed somewhere east of the Missouri River. That would be too ordinary.

"If I could sit down to a table at the best hotel in the land," he said, "I'd prefer to eat the dinner that I'm going to cook for you fellows tomorrow."

Williams sneered. "Yes," he said, "we put old Tex" — a long-horn bull — "out of his starving misery, and the boys have found his liver to be O.K. Maybe you can give us a liver pie."

"I'll do better than that," said the boy; "I'll not only give you a beef stew, but a pudding that you can't buy outside of London or Liverpool — a plum duff — and a cake. Old Tex will also be on the menu in several places, for his tenderloin looks good, and there are a few steaks which, when properly treated with a maul on the top of a stump, will be as good as you will get in a 'Frisco water-front lodging, and better than any of you fellows have had since we hit the drifts."

I have eaten meals that mother used to cook, I've been famished during a sea voyage, and have devoured a Norwegian sailor's pea soup; I've participated in several real banquets in New York; I've dined at Delmonico's and at Sherry's, at Young's in Boston, and I've feasted in a circus-cook tent; but my Christmas dinner in the foothills of Wyoming in 1873, under the circumstances I have but faintly described, still is a fond memory and holds the record as the best meal I ever ate. It was as follows:

Menu

Marrowbone Soup — "Tex"   Water Cress
                    Beef Stew — "Tex"
                 Hamburg Steak — "Tex"
            Planked Porterhouse Steak — "Tex"
Tenderloin Steak — "Tex"   Roast Beef — "Tex"
        Corn Bread   Wheat Bread
        English Plum Pudding — Hard and Soft Sauce
            Raisins   Cake   Coffee   Tea
(No butter or milk)   (Lots of salt and pepper)

The corn bread was made from meal milled by the cook from shelled corn in the cargo. The "plums" were raisins, of which the cook had a few pounds. He used wheat flour, baking powder, and grease saved from the final ration of the bacon which gave out a week before Christmas. The hard sauce was made with sugar and grease and a flavoring extract. The soft or liquid sauce contained a "remedy" requisitioned from a homeopathic quantity found in the wagon boss's medicine chest — a few spoonfuls of brandy. The water cress was found two miles away at a spring. The boys called it "pepper grass." There it was fresh and green, protected by spring water which never freezes, and in some places it was peeping out from the edge of the snow at the brook side.

And now about whisky. There were sixty men in this camp, and in one of the big wagons were three barrels of whisky, but it belonged to the post trader at Fort Fetterman, and it was a tradition not even broken on this exceptional passage from Medicine Bow on the

U. P. to Fort Fetterman on the North Platte that a
consignment of hard liquor was as safe in a bull train
as it would be anywhere on earth, and that it would
reach its destination untouched. Few men drank intoxi-
cants on these trips. It was a crime to be found with
whisky, punishable by banishment from camp, and that
might have meant death. But at both ends of the
journey — that's another story.

The plainsman and mountaineer, the bullwhacker and
the stage driver, when chilled, drank water. Whisky
caused him to perspire, and that was bad. He did not
often use it when on duty.

One of the peculiar things about this Christmas dinner
is the fact that there were no mountain grouse, no sage
hen, no antelope, deer, or elk for the menu. The truth
is, the storm drove everything of the kind in another
direction — the direction in which we were slowly moving — and some time later, when we emerged upon the
other side of the range with our ox-power so greatly
reduced that we made less than a mile of progress a
day, the herds of elk stampeded a dozen times past our
camps, and the "fool grouse" sat a dozen in a group
upon the pine boughs in the mountains and refused to
move, allowing us to kill them, if so disposed, one at a
time; but we did it only once, just to prove that it
could be done.

It took us a couple of weeks to shovel our way out,
and while the sun shone in the middle of the day, hardly
a flake of the snow melted. The air was at times biting
cold, but invigorating, and every man, including the
boss and the cook and even the night-herder, fell to the
work with a will that finally meant victory. In places
we operated in the drifts as you see the excavators in a
city cellar or subway operate, digging down to the surface

and then benching as the open-ground miners or cellar excavators do, the men below tossing the blocks of snow up to the bench above and they in turn passing it to the top of the drift.

Once or twice, in narrow passages, it was necessary to build several benches. In one place we began to tunnel but the plan was given up, for our wagons, the regulation prairie schooners, would require a passage big enough for a railroad furniture car to pass through.

After the high plateau was reached — the land that represented the watershed of the Platte Valley — it was clear sailing, and while food — wild game — was plentiful, and we ate lots of it, the memory of our Christmas dinner remained to remind us, after all, that in the midst of greatest hardships and suffering we often find something to be thankful for, something to bring us to our senses when we grumble or complain of our ill luck or misfortunes.

Had I been as appreciative when I partook of this mountain dinner as I am today for the blessings of Divine Providence, I should have been able to say, in relating this story, that we properly gave thanks to Him who is responsible for all our blessings and who chasteneth us for our wickedness; but I was not properly appreciative, nor were my rough but honest companions. Therefore, I take this opportunity to say grace just fifty years late:

Thank God for that snowbound Christmas dinner.

"'What's the damage, Fritz?'"

CHAPTER SIXTEEN

THE BULLWHACKERS' JUBILEE

IT WAS while a bull outfit was loading for one of the
fall trips to Fetterman that the first billiard table came
to Medicine Bow. I think it was the only one in the
Territory, outside of Cheyenne and Laramie City, both
division points on the Union Pacific. There were no
women in Medicine Bow, good or bad, at the time, and
not more than a hundred regular residents; yet the
town had a saloon, because the bull outfits — Hunton's
and others — in their occasional trips, and a few adven-
turers who were prospecting south and west of the
"Bow," furnished ample patronage to make the enter-
prise profitable. It was this saloon keeper who conceived
the idea of importing a billiard table, and also a back
bar and mirror.

The bullwhackers watched the installation of the new
furniture, and that night informed the saloon keeper

that as there were no women in the camp, it had been decided to have a "stag dance" in the saloon. He protested, but it did no good. A few drinks in a dozen leaders was followed by a deliberately aimed shot which shattered the mirror, after which the operation of removing the billiard table began. It was a rough job, and would have given a Brunswick-Balke man a chill. The table went out on to the prairie in sections, and the sections were not always separated at the regulation point. The green cover was ruined.

Then the dance began. The German saloon keeper smiled his protests, but when he became too much concerned about what was going on, some one would snuff a light or plug a barrel of whisky with a bullet. So the night's debauch continued, and it did not end until daybreak. The place was a wreck, and the saloon keeper was in despair when the wagon boss came along with a roll of money as big around as a ship's cable, saying:

"What's the damage, Fritz?"

"Ach," he replied, "the table cost me $500; a barrel of whisky, and cigars, beer, my fine mirror — everyding is gone!"

"Yes, I see; the whole bizness," said the boss.

"Well," said Fritz, "the boys spent $600 mit me, so I make it $600 more; maybe I can mend the table."

So the bill was paid, the wagons were loaded, and the outfit sallied forth across the plains, the bridgeless rivers, and the mountain passes to Fetterman, where there was a pay day. Deductions pro rata were made from every man's wage to even up the score with Fritz, and every bullwhacker paid his share willingly, saying it was cheap sport for the price. There was no feeling against Fritz, because Fritz had not shown fight. If he had — well, most of the men in the outfit were wild and woolly, and rough, but not killers. Still, one or two could not be trusted.

It is not difficult for a person to understand why these wild celebrations would occur if he will pause to picture the hard, lonely, and often dangerous life the bullwhacker had to lead on the trail. When the freighters finally did get back to town after a joyless season in the wilderness, all their pent-up energy would generally burst forth in madly extravagant recreation of the rough-and-tough sort provided by those who lay in wait for his hard-earned dollars.

The long trip over the desert gave most of the bull-whackers unquenchable thirst; and sometimes it created strange appetites that were hard to appease. I recall such an appetite I had found on one trip. For nearly a year at one time I was beyond the sound of a bell, the whistle of a locomotive, the tick of a clock. During this period I had not had a taste of sugar, pie, cake, or vegetables, excepting white beans. In that time, strangely enough, I did not acquire a dislike of either beans or bacon, my principal diet, but rather formed a lifelong appetite for them. But there was one thing that I constantly craved that heretofore had not been a particularly favorite article of food with me, and it may interest you to know what I did about it when, finally, I landed in Cheyenne.

Unyoking my team at a camp on Crow Creek, I immediately started for town with the rest of the bull-whackers, and listened with deep interest to their plans as we trudged along afoot. Every one had a pocketful of money, some of them several months' pay, and we were all like a lot of sailors just ashore from a trip around the world.

One of the men had already divided into two separate

rolls the money he planned to spend: he had in one pocket $20 for a suit of clothes; the rest, about $100, was in a wad in another pocket. This he said was his "jubilee fund"; he intended to spend every cent of it for two days of wild life.

An older man tried to induce him to go with him to a bank and open an account. Instead of doing that, the improvident bullwhacker sat down beside the trail, took out both rolls, and looked them over. Finally, he transferred a five-dollar bill from his clothing to the jubilee fund, saying he could buy all the clothes he wanted for $15. Before we reached the Tracey corral on the outskirts of Cheyenne, he had put all his money into the jubilee fund except $2.50, with which, he said, he could buy a good pair of overalls and a blouse.

There was only one idea in my head. I had no taste for liquor, neither was I madly anxious to find a gaming table or a good restaurant. I wanted *onions*, and onions I intended to have — also a lot of them. I had not laid hands or eyes on an onion for nearly a year, and while I never had cared much for them, my onion appetite, as I walked toward Cheyenne and as I entered the first street, was almost overpowering. So I began immediately to look for a place where they were for sale. I soon came to a large outfitting warehouse, where I found in large quantities what I wanted.

At this point I left the little party, bought a peck of onions, large and small ones, and returned to camp, which I found deserted by every one but the nightherder, who had just crawled out of a wagon.

Building a fire, I put on some water and in a few minutes had a dozen onions cooking. Then I peeled a couple of big ones, got out the salt and a pone of bread, and ate my fill of raw ones. The night-herder joined me and helped enjoy the feast. I also fried and ate a lot of them, and when I again started for Cheyenne, my craving for onions had been subdued. But my appetite for this humble "fruit" has never been wholly appeased, and the onion has never ceased to be a favorite.

Later in the day I ran across the bullwhacker who had set aside $2.50 for a pair of overalls and a blouse. True to the determination reached on the way to town, he had invested that sum and appeared in his new togs. Also he had made the rounds of the saloons and dives and was dizzy from drink. The next day found him at camp penniless. Several companions were with him, all in the same condition — "heap sick" and "dead broke," dependent on good old Nath Williams for their bacon, bread, and coffee, and perfectly willing to look after the cattle, watch the property of the outfit, and wait for it to start again for the north.

"I hailed him, at the same time half raising my rifle."

CHAPTER SEVENTEEN

A WINTER IN A DUGOUT

THE winter of 1874–1875 I spent in a dugout built in an embankment of La Bonte Creek two hundred and fifty miles northwest of Cheyenne, at a point a couple of miles from the old Oregon Trail. My partner was Nicholas Huber, a man old enough to be my grandfather, and he had been in the army so long that he knew but little of anything except soldiering. He had little use for the rest of the human family, and I believe many times wished that I would get lost or desert him.

Nick was not by any means a bad man — far from it, and I liked him; but his army life had made him a grouch and he was embittered against society generally. Anyway, he swore he never would live in a town again, and I believe he kept his vow. On the other hand, while I had nothing against the settlements or the rest of humanity, I thought more of adventure than I did of what I could find in cities, or where other people

106

congregated in numbers. In fact, I rather prided myself in being a sort of Robinson Crusoe, and actually tried to induce Nick to be my man Friday.

It was due to my lack of diplomacy in broaching this subject to old Nick that we nearly parted company. In truth, he threatened to set me adrift if I ever again made any pretension to being the master of the manor. He was boss, he said, and not I.

I did not agree to this. The consequence was that we passed weeks at a time together without speaking. At times I sincerely believed that poor old Nick had lost his mind. As we slept in bunks only a few feet apart I sometimes put in restless nights, being afraid to sleep soundly for fear that he might in an insane moment kill me. I never went to bed without placing my rifle lengthwise in the bed under my buffalo robes and blankets, besides having my pistol handy. That was his habit, too; and sometimes it looked pretty warlike, for Nick had a habit of mumbling to himself and glaring at me, especially just before we retired for the night.

Often we tried to outsit one another; and neither would give up until sleep drove us to bed. I was usually the first to arise, stir up the coals and start a good fire, and get the coffee and bacon going.

It was a miserable feeling to be housed together and to be so unsocial. Many times I tried to resume conversation with the old man, but it was next to impossible to get him to reply.

Things had gone on in this way for fully two weeks, when one night Nick suddenly found his speech through a rather dramatic occurrence. About midnight I was awakened by a shock that seemed to rock the cabin. At the same time Nick awoke, for by the light of the coals in the fireplace I saw him sit up.

"Did you hear a noise?" I ventured, as he rolled over.

"Yes," he responded; "it was either an earthquake or an explosion. Maybe Laramie Peak has erupted; look and see."

Then I arose and pushed aside the double thickness of gunny sacks we used as a door, the bottom part of which was loaded with boulders to keep it from blowing open. There was no light from the direction of the peak, and I so reported. We were stumped, and discussed the matter for an hour. Nick went to sleep, but I kept awake, waiting for the first sign of daybreak. Then, quietly arising, I shouldered my gun and went downstream, following its winding course on the ice. Later on Nick arose, saw my trail in the snow, and went up-creek. I walked about half a mile without seeing anything to rouse my suspicions, when suddenly I felt a presence, though I heard not a sound. It is strange but true that some of us — most of us, I believe — who lived on the wild frontier possessed this instinct or faculty, whatever it is, and I cannot explain it. I was sure that some one was about, and as I knew the locality as well as a householder knows his own dooryard, I crept silently forward, knowing that I was approaching a parklike spot in the bottoms, a sort of meadow bordered by heavy undergrowth. When I came to the opening, daylight was breaking clearly; and as I spread a bunch of dry branches to get a look into the opening, I saw standing a few rods away a man dressed in buckskin, his right hand resting on his chin and his left hand under his right elbow, evidently in a solemn, contemplative mood. It was Bob Yaeger, at that time well known in the wilder parts of Wyoming.

I hailed him, at the same time half raising my rifle in his direction and stepping out in full view.

"Hello!" I shouted, "what's doing?"

"I'm friendly," he said calmly, "but in a heap o' trouble. My powder exploded, a whole can of it, and blew my Sibley tent, grub, and everything I had to pieces."

I then approached, for I already saw the wreck. There were pieces of buffalo robe, canvas, and tent poles everywhere, while blankets hung on the bushes, and they and the limbs were splattered with what I took to be bloody pieces of flesh.

"Any one with you?" I asked.

"Nobody," he replied.

"Well, what's this on the bushes — looks like meat. Did you have a critter?"

Bob Yaeger laughed and informed me that what I took to be the entrails of a human being was nothing more or less than tomatoes, a case of which in cans had been blown hither and yon.

Yaeger had come out the night before to this spot to cut some big logs of cottonwood into cordwood for the Fort Laramie commissary, and the powder was to be used for blasting the gnarled and frozen timber, for every cottonwood tree in the La Bonte bottoms was dead, soaked and frozen. Yaeger explained that he had been hauled to the spot with his outfit, including a grindstone, by a four-mule team and a soldier teamster who had immediately returned to the fort about forty miles to the northwest. Even the grindstone had been blown far from the tent. Explaining the explosion, he said that when he retired he had left the flap of the tent up on the side from which the wind came at midnight, and that it had blown the coals from his fire against the big can of powder; and the first thing he knew, the tent and contents, including the blankets over him, were up in the air. He himself had escaped miraculously, not having a powder mark.

Yaeger was very friendly, and while he generously gave me a can of tomatoes and a can of corn that were undamaged, I found an empty can which I filled with tomato pulp I harvested from near-by bushes. It was precious stuff that I hadn't tasted in months.

After we had gathered his scattered camp as best we could, Bob went with me to our dugout and had breakfast. Old Nick had got over his grouch and talked freely to this first visitor to our camp.

"With his jackknife he had fashioned a jumping-jack and a whistle."

CHAPTER EIGHTEEN

OLD NICK'S CHRISTMAS BIRTHDAY

OUR La Bonte Creek dugout was located two hundred and forty miles from the other end of the trail at Cheyenne. Along the way were only Hunton's, — more than a hundred miles from the lodge, — and closer to Cheyenne several other adobe or log "stations," including Clay's, Macfarlane's, one at Bear Springs, and finally a plastered adobe at Horse Creek. La Bonte Lodge, therefore, was a long way from civilization, if Fort Fetterman and a handful of soldiers at the mouth of La Prele Creek are not included.

From the doorway of La Bonte Lodge — when the gunny sacks used as a door were moved to one side and draped over a wooden peg driven into the log doorframe for the purpose — there was, on clear days, a grand view of Laramie Peak, a saw-toothed mountain that pierced the clouds when there were any to pierce,

111

which was not often. Just below the doorway, in the
deep bottom of the creek, were monster cottonwoods,
every one of them dead and as white as though they
had been calcimined. In between these monarchs had
grown many gnarled box elders. There were no pines.
But away off yonder, on Laramie Peak, whose blue
outlines showed against the sky, there were great forests
of "Christmas trees"; and this was what made the
peak so blue, their number being massed into a great
blanket except at the top, where snow furnished a pure
white crown for the great mountain nine or ten months
of the year.

Standing in the doorway in late December, I said to
Nick: "Wonder how far it is to the peak yonder?"

Nick left the bean pot which he was stirring and, coming to the door, gazed off for a moment toward the
biggest peak in the Lower Black Hills and said:

"If I had a contract to haul freight with bull teams
to the foot of Laramie Peak, I should want to be paid
on a mileage of sixty, at least. And, as the grades are
largely up from this point, I should want at least four
cents a pound if I hauled from La Bonte Creek and
broke the trail, which, of course, I would have to do,
because there isn't a mile of trail between here and
there."

"Well, Nick," I continued, "do you suppose there's a
small pine tree anywhere between here and the peak —
one that could be used for a Christmas tree?"

"Oh, sure; there are some not twenty miles from
here over toward the Medicine Bow; and then back
along La Prele Creek, perhaps eighteen miles from this
cabin, there are lots of scrub pines; but what do you
want with a Christmas tree? We haven't anything to
put on it, and no one to see it but us; are you crazy?"

"I said to Nick: 'Wonder how far it is to the peak yonder?'"

"No, I'm not crazy at all; but I thought it would be nice for us to have a tree, and put on it a few things we could fix up, say for Christmas Eve."

"Well, that's not a bad idea, Bill. . . . When is Christmas? What day of the month is today? Give me the date." And he laughed.

I admitted that I didn't know, and that I hadn't seen a calendar for over a year, and had lost track entirely of the days of the week and the days of the month; but both of us knew it was December, or at least thought so. But we had no way of settling the matter unless a stray hunter should happen along, an event that had not occurred since snow began to fall several weeks before. It was not an unusual thing for frontiersmen to lose all reckoning of days and dates.

"You settle the date," finally said Huber, "and I'll furnish the tree, if I have to pack it from the peak. We'll find something to decorate it with."

That night, while the back log in the dugout fireplace burned low, I lay in my bunk wide awake after Nick had entered dreamland, thinking, thinking how I could find out when Christmas Day would be at hand; but I fell asleep without making the slightest progress. I believed we had started work on the dugout about the first of October; but I hadn't a good reason for so believing because, when I was told by Jack Hunton that the season's freighting from the railroad at Cheyenne to the North Platte was closed and that I had best dig in somewhere for the winter where antelope and other game were plentiful, I was no wiser as to dates than I was now in trying to decide when to celebrate the Nativity.

It was a forty-mile walk to Fort Fetterman, the trail (the old Oregon) was practically obliterated, and in places there were drifts and bad traveling prospects generally. But when I arose in the morning, I said: "Nick, I'm going to the fort and find out when Christmas is due, and I'm going to start after breakfast, unless you object."

"Why should I object?" queried Nick. "I have a greater reason for wanting to observe Christmas than you have; it means more to me than it does to you."

"How's that?"

"Never mind; tallow your boots, pack your kit, and be off. I'll tell you all about it when we have found the Christmas tree."

So I started for Fetterman. It was a bitter cold day, and the thermometer — a thing neither of us had seen in several seasons — must have registered away below zero, for the air was full of nipping frost that bit at my ears and fingers. But the traveling was better than I expected it to be, the cold spell having frozen the earlier falls of snow into hard crusts over which, much of the way, I trotted like an Indian, maintaining a steady, easy swing. At noon I camped at Bedtick Creek, where there was a bubbling spring, and ate my bacon and bread and warmed over the cooked venison I had brought along, using a willow stick. I had made about eighteen miles, a little more than five miles an hour, and was not at all fatigued.

At eight that night I climbed the short hill to the post trader's log house just inside the fort, where I found a number of civilian friends who had foregathered for a quiet game of poker and a few drinks. Every one was surprised to see me, and Post Trader Tillotson wanted to know if "Old Nick," as he significantly called him, had driven me out. I assured him that nothing of the kind had happened, and explained that I needed a few things, including thread, needles, green coffee berries, a skinning knife, and so forth.

"By George," I said to Tillotson, "just to show you that Nick and I are on good terms — at present — I am buying him this knife as a Christmas present."

Tillotson smiled, twisted his thumb to a small calendar hanging back of the bar, and said, "Well, young man, you'd better make it a New Year's gift, because today is Christmas."

That night I cuddled to a campfire in one blanket down among the box elders at the creek, for there was no such thing as sleeping in the fort; in fact, I was lucky to be allowed inside at all, because most so-called civilians were none too popular with the army men; but after the lapse of all these years I am not at all inclined to find fault with their judgment. Men like Hunton, of course, were welcome, for they were filling contracts and had standing.

It might be imagined that Mr. Tillotson would be surprised to discover that I didn't know that it was Christmas, but he never cracked a smile, and the men at the card table said not a word.

My trip back to La Bonte was much slower and more laborious, for besides my gun and blanket I carried at least sixty pounds of stuff I had bought from the post trader. I took my time and spent a night by a campfire at a point about halfway, not turning in, however, until late and rising at break of day. I left Fetterman at sunup on the twenty-seventh and reached La Bonte at sundown on the twenty-eighth.

Dropping my pack at the cabin, I drew aside the gunny sacks, and there stood Nick beside a small pine tree that he had decorated with paper flowers made from soap wrappers — white, brown, and red; and with his

jackknife he had fashioned a jumping-jack and a whistle,
which he smilingly announced — and with, for him, rare
good nature — were for "one good boy." My mouth
opened to tell him the truth, but it closed quickly when
the thought flashed through my mind, "Why disappoint
him? Why not tell him today is Christmas?" And I
did.

"All right," said Nick; "then you may congratulate
me, for this is my sixty-fifth birthday."

Nick Huber was handy with a jackknife or any edged
tool, I soon discovered, for he proceeded to make a
number of other "presents" and decorations for the
tree, informing me quite volubly, as soon as he had
swallowed the first mouthful from the pint bottle I set
before him, that as a boy he had worked in his father's
toy factory at Nürnberg, Bavaria, and that he had run
away from home and came to America, eventually en-
listing in the United States Army.

Whether Nick Huber ever discovered that he cele-
brated his birthday three days late or not I cannot
say; but when I deceived him, I believed it would have
been as cruel to tell the truth as it would to destroy a
child's belief in the existence of Santa Claus.

The old soldier did have a heart in him, after all.
We got along very well when we had come to know each
other better. I think there was no more trouble between
us during the rest of our stay in the old dugout.

We broke up camp early in the spring rather suddenly,
when a beaver trapper who happened along told us he
was headed south because another trapper had told him
the Sioux were coming across the Platte. They were
out to kill anything in the shape of a white man they
could find.

We were ready to go, and we went in a hurry, Nick

heading for Fort Laramie and I for Fetterman, where I camped for a while outside the fort. Later on I trudged over the Medicine Bow range and plains to the railroad, and finally to Laramie City and Sherman on the summit of the Lower Black Hills, where I had friends. They had not heard from me for so long a time that they thought me dead.

"They singled out a steer and snubbed him to a wagon wheel."

CHAPTER NINETEEN

THE BATTLE WITH THE LONGHORNS

ONE of my most exciting experiences on the old freight trails began with the yoking up of a herd of wild steers just off the Texas range, — longhorns three and four years old. These cattle not only had never been yoked, but until within a few days had never spent a minute in a corral or had any closer contact with a man than was necessary when a cowboy threw them and burned monograms of cattle barons into their hides. Men, to these cattle, were things to be avoided, and the sight of a man was usually a signal for a quick movement to some other place.

Nevertheless, Pratt and Farris had closed a contract with the United States government for hauling several thousand tons of provisions to the Red Cloud and Spotted Tail agencies, some two hundred miles north. This old Sidney Trail ran through the sand hills of western Nebraska.

The contractors were unprepared with motive power.

119

Broken bulls could not be bought in sufficient numbers, no matter what prices were offered, anywhere west of the Missouri River. It was clear that something heroic must be attempted, and what they attempted was surely heroic. For two days thirty of us battled with the wild Texas longhorns in a great corral of about sixty wagons — all new Shuttlers, as I remember.

I am reporting the event for the first time as a matter of record, and am prepared to say that few other happenings in my life are clearer in my mind; consequently I am sure that what I say here is correct. Not a casualty can be reported so far as the thirty bullwhackers are concerned, although not a few bulls lost their horns, others were blinded, and others cruelly lassoed, choked, beaten, dragged, and yoked and chained. Two or three and sometimes a half-dozen men singled out for attack a handsome steer with a yard or more sweep of horn and snubbed him to a wagon wheel, soon providing him with a mate with whom he could, and usually did, fight until they both tired of it.

New cattle just being trained to yoke were always put in the center of the team, where they were easily managed with the assistance of the "leaders," which were always light weights and almost always longhorns from Texas — long horns, long legs and bodies, thin as razor-back hogs. These leaders were always the best-broken oxen, and would respond to the low-spoken word of "haw" or "gee," especially if the word were uttered in the peculiar musical tone of the whacker. This cannot be described in print, not only because it is impossible to convey sound in that manner, but because the language that goes with the music — the request to gee or haw — would not be pleasant reading. Alone, the leaders would trot like horses.

The average person outside of Texas and the South-west and some of the Western states has a mental picture, perhaps, of the Texas steer of the longhorn variety. Those who lived thirty or forty years ago, even in the East, remember him as a member of the quadruped family consisting largely of horn, for it was not an infrequent thing to see him in a cattle car on a sidetrack. He was, as a matter of fact, also entitled to a reputation for his legs, for they were unusually long. His body, too, was slim, and he never was fat for the reason that while free to roam the ranges at will, he devoted most of his time to using his horns in goring his mates and neglected to eat. He raced about from place to place, whereas, if he had had no horns, he would have been a peaceful animal and consequently much more valuable for the market.

The old-time Texas steer often was as fleet-footed as a Kentucky racehorse of the thoroughbred variety, and it took a good horse to catch him when he made up his mind to run. Nevertheless, thousands of these Texas steers were broken to yoke and used in overland trans-portation; and, once broken, they were good workers, even though their horns were always in the way and the cause of a great deal of trouble in a herd.

While I have no authority for the statement, I believe that practical dehorning began with the bullwhackers of the plains, for they frequently bored holes in the horns and this in a few weeks caused the horns to drop off. Then it was noted that if the dehorned cattle were kept separate from those with horns, the dehorned ones, even when working hard every day, took on flesh and were better workers. Finally, nearly all the work-oxen were dehorned, and they were as meek and quiet as lambs.

When the Pratt and Farris bull train of longhorns

finally strung out along the Sidney Trail, which ran up the center coulee of the bluff on the north side of the Union Pacific tracks on to the famous so-called Sidney Crossing of the North Platte, and then on to the northern wilderness, it was the wildest-looking outfit of the kind any one of us had ever seen.

There were few of us who ever expected to finish the trek, for before we had moved a mile, some of the poor steers were either lying in the dust of the trail or were being dragged by the few trained bulls that were scattered through the various teams. Others had been choked to death, and in at least one case a fine Texan steer, once the possessor of two great horns, was a poor, bleeding, dying creature beside the road, one of his horns having been broken off.

We made less than three miles the first lap of the trip. It took us hours to hook up when we did get ready to proceed the second day, even though all the wild steers were left yoked together and turned out to fight between themselves until, sometimes, one or the other would succumb. But Charley Moore, the wagon boss, had prepared for these eventualities, having brought along a big drove of other steers to take the places of those he knew would be killed.

The newly yoked steers did little grazing the first time they were turned loose, pulling and hauling and trying desperately to free themselves from their imprisonment — but never with success, unless they broke their necks in the attempt. This thing continued, I believe, for a week, before we reached Sidney Crossing.

The bullwhackers had been mostly recruited from Cheyenne, and while they were a rough-and-ready-looking crew, most of them were honest, hard-working, and sober men. However, there were two or three, as is usually the case, who had bad records, mostly with their pistols — one in particular named Ed Patterson, nicknamed "One-eyed Ed."

We found the old fording approach at the river washed out. This meant a lot of hard work, for there was a considerable embankment to be cut down and prepared with logs to carry the heavy loads over the soft earth. Moore planned for us to reach this place in the evening, so that we should have a whole day from sunup to sundown to ford the wide stream. As I remember, or thought at the time, it was nearly a mile across, including an island of sand in the center upon which there was a growth of underbrush, including some young ash. From this ash I cut several whipstocks.

Both the south and north channels contained quicksand, but the water was at a low stage and in no place on the entire crossing more than waist deep to a bullwhacker or belly deep to a bull. We doubled teams on each pair of wagons, lead and trail.

Our cargo consisted largely of unsacked bacon, some brown sugar, and flour — the flour being the dirtiest stuff I ever saw under that name. The bacon was filled with sand that drifted upon it.

As I remember, we did not raise the wagon boxes at all. Anyway, there was little to be injured by water, and I guess no one cared much about that, for the stuff was for so-called Indian braves whom no one in Nebraska, Wyoming, or Dakota at that time considered were entitled to what little they did get for their land. Surely none of us had much sympathy for any Indian; and whenever the topic was discussed the government was roundly scored for sending anything to them at all, the idea being that there should be a wholesale war of extermination, in which we should all be invited to participate.

Of course, I have since changed my mind, which I am glad to say has had time to mature and understand.

It was about four o'clock in the afternoon of that late October day that we dragged the last wagon of the outfit across the Platte, and we had much less trouble with the new bulls than we expected. By this time nearly all of them had quieted down, some of them to steady work, filling their yokes and calmly submitting to handling by the bullwhackers. I had five yoke (of my team of seven yoke) of really fine cattle, and took great pains with them and did not mistreat them at all. The result was that I had very little trouble, and before I left the outfit, which I did at Red Cloud, as I shall detail later on, they were thoroughly trained and were yoked and unyoked with comparative ease and without much resistance after leaving the Platte Valley.

We corralled on a flat surface of the wide bottom. This was not low land or land that had ever, apparently, overflowed, because the mounds of a prairie-dog town were there, although uninhabited at the time.

"Patterson took deliberate aim and pressed the trigger."

CHAPTER TWENTY

THE FATE OF "ONE-EYED ED"[1]

Our sixty wagons made a great corral, and the messes were started without delay, while every one except those who were assigned to the camp kettles was told off into crews to work with jacks and levers raising and greasing every wheel in the train. I was assigned to two large pots of beans which were to be eaten the next day, while several other whackers were sent to the frying-pans and bacon and the coffee pots.

Just as I had my pots well boiling, "One-eyed Ed" came up to me. I saw at the first glance that he had been drinking. He asked me if I knew he was a dead shot. I told him I hadn't known him long enough to know what he could do or couldn't do, but that if he said he could shoot straight, he was probably telling the truth, because nearly all of us knew how to do that.

[1] The "One-eyed Ed" story as it appeared in "The Prairie Schooner" is a somewhat different version, but this was due to a desire at that time (1918) to keep my own personality out of what I was writing about the West. The present version is in every respect a correct account of a famous tragedy at a one-time famous fording place on the North Platte. *W. F. H.*

125

Secretly I had some doubts, because he had but one eye, the ball being entirely gone from one socket.

He suspected that I was more or less incredulous; therefore he insisted that we have an exhibition, and that I throw up some targets in the shape of old tin cans that littered this regular camp ground, and that he would "pink every one of them on the wing." I allowed that I had to watch the bean pots, and he would have to excuse me until some other time; but "no" wouldn't do for an answer, and he lifted the pots off the fire, pointed his gun at my head, and ordered me to throw a tin can in the air. This I did without further argument, and before it had gone many feet above my head he bored a neat hole through it.

He continued this for some time, and I noticed that Moore, who rode by on his big horse, was a witness to what was going on, and he made no objections. Finally Patterson insisted that I toss two cans at a time, and I did. He perforated both of them, and within a few minutes he was shooting the cans out of my hands as fast as I could pick them up. Finally I protested and refused to toss up any more cans, and he put a bullet through my sombrero, grazing my thick mop of hair. Not a soul of the crowd that had formed about us made a protest, but I could see that several of the fellows were worried and were afraid that he would kill me. I kept cool and never lost my head.

Patterson had two revolvers, big Remingtons or Colts, and when he put one of them aside and brought out the other from his belt, I determined to play the game to the end and do it as pleasantly as possible; but I had a plan, and it worked, but not until an hour or so later. In the meantime I had a rest and continued with my bean job.

Moore, who seemed to know Patterson pretty well, sent him out in the bottoms east of camp with instructions to kill some veal in the herd that was being ranged there by a Texas contracting company for the Red Cloud Agency. He soon returned with the veal, but he also had the hearts and livers of several three- or four-year-old steers. These he put on a tailboard, and with a butcher knife chopped them into cubes.

Then it struck Patterson that he ought to have another session of marksmanship with me as William Tell's son; so he arose and ordered me to resume, which I did. I soon saw that he had only three or four cartridges in his pistol, and that the other was empty. His Winchester had been left in a sling on his wagon box in the other wing of the corral. I had located that. So the moment I saw that he had no more charges in his revolver, I quietly reached for my Springfield, which I had purposely stood up against a wheel near the campfire, and leveled it at his head, saying:

"This thing has gone as far as it is going to. Let me alone, or I will defend myself in the only way I can."

He was a miserable coward, and I was immediately surrounded by a half-dozen good fellows who also interceded, and he finally went away, as I verily believe, to get his Winchester or load his revolvers for me. But fate had not decided upon me for his victim, but upon another, and at that time a much more prominent and valuable citizen. The man who was in charge of the beef herd at that moment rode into the north end of the wagon corral on a splendid black horse with a white diamond in his forehead and a left front white fetlock.

Moore met this man, a fine-looking Texan, dressed in every way to play the part of a boss herder, with an expensive saddle under him, and wearing a Texas sombrero.

"Hello, Charley," he shouted.

"Hello, Bob," replied Moore, "how are you?"

"I'm pretty hot, Moore," he went on, "because some one from your outfit has been out in one of my herds and killed several fine critters. Aren't you satisfied with veal? You know I am glad to have you kill all the calves you want, but —"

He never finished that sentence, for in the meantime Patterson, his heart filled with murder, — possibly having made up his mind to kill me, — stepped upon one of the dead prairie-dog mounds, whipped out his revolver, took deliberate aim, and, as one of the men shouted, "Don't shoot! Don't shoot!" pressed the trigger.

Bob Porter had heard the warning cry and turned his head slightly to see what was going on, just in time to receive Patterson's bullet behind his right ear. It passed clean through his head. His arms went into the air, his horse lunged forward, and in a second the man, who a moment before was in good health, lay dead on the ground with his face upturned and eyes half closed.

I ran to the black charger, which, trembling and snorting, stood looking at his murdered master, took off the bridle, substituted a halter, and tied the now sweating animal to a wagon wheel. In the meantime a dozen men had surrounded Patterson, including Moore.

Patterson was sober and pale, and his hand shook as Moore chided him for his crime, saying: "You fool! That bunch across the river will be over here after you and perhaps shoot all of us up for this thing. You'd better get out and lose no time about it!"

So Patterson, with his Winchester over his shoulder, started up river, while Moore waited until he had gone perhaps a half mile and then, mounting his horse, plunged into the water and headed for the island to cross over to the cow camp, which was on the other side but some distance from our fording place, to notify Porter's friends of what had happened.

I will say, to keep this record straight, that I did not go away and hide or keep out of Patterson's sight after he committed this foul crime. Neither did any one else. In fact, we all protested in his presence against allowing him to go at all, and I held my gun handy while I faced both Patterson and Moore and said what I had to say. I had been badly treated, and I verily believed that I was Patterson's intended victim, for apparently it mattered not at all whom he killed. He was full of blood lust and was looking for a victim.

But Patterson was as yellow as saffron — I mean his heart; for his face was ashen white, and his legs and hands trembled, and his fingers twitched as he stood dumbly fumbling his mustache, thinking the matter over and demanding a horse from Moore, which Moore refused to let him have; and I say this at this late day because there never was a trial as a result of this foul crime, and because I afterward heard it said at Cheyenne that Moore and Porter were enemies and that Moore had told Patterson to shoot. That is not so. He did nothing of the kind, and I say this in face of the fact that Moore treated me shamefully a few weeks later, as he did others, by deserting us at White River, nearly two hundred miles from the nearest railroad or settlement.

From up the river Patterson saw that Moore had started to cross over to the other side and notify the cow camp; so he ran along the shore and finally plunged into the water and tried to head Moore off on the long sand island, but never got in range. However, Patterson found himself between two hostile forces, the bull-whackers on one side and the cowboys on the other, and he was soon surrounded, captured, and taken prisoner to the cow camp. It was now night, and before leaving to notify Porter's friends, Moore instructed me and a negro not to take our eyes off the corpse. I threw a clean blanket over the body and covered the face with a bandanna handkerchief. It was a pretty cool night, and we built a dung fire, dragged up a couple of yokes, and sat there all night to keep off any wild animals that might be prowling about. As a matter of fact, the coyotes howled almost continuously throughout the night, and once or twice came so near us that we pelted them with small pebbles and they scampered away.

That very night Patterson was securely roped, placed on the back of a horse, and, accompanied by a large number of cowboys, started for Sidney, about forty miles south. However, before this posse started, a messenger on a fleet horse had been despatched ahead. He stopped at Jim Reddington's ranch a few miles west of the Sidney Trail, and word was sent from there to several ranches south and near the railroad to friends of Porter, and by the time the posse and prisoner reached Sidney, it is said that at least two hundred horsemen were there to meet them. The prisoner was escorted down the middle coulee or washout, while from the other two — one on either side — came the avengers. A lasso was thrown over the prisoner's head by one of Porter's friends, its coil tightened around his waist, — not his neck, — and he was dragged to a telegraph pole. A detail of soldiers from Fort McPherson came upon the scene after Patterson had paid the penalty for his crime, but they made no attempt to interfere. In fact, they did not even cut the body down, and it remained hanging at the end of the rawhide lariat for twenty-four hours, the lariat stretching until the knees of the mob's victim rested on the ground.

Before Patterson was hanged he was asked if he had anything to say, and he admitted that he had killed, a short time before, two soldiers for the purpose of robbery.

The next night there arrived in our camp several horsemen and a couple of men driving a team of horses attached to a light wagon. They took the body of Porter to Sidney.

"The Indian was demanding a side of bacon and a bull."

CHAPTER TWENTY–ONE

THE RETURN FROM RED CLOUD

WE resumed our trek to Red Cloud over an almost obliterated trail. The soil was sandy and broken into hills, washouts, and lowlands, and our progress was very slow — not more than a mile or two for several days. There was mush ice in every stream, and woe be to the bullwhacker who had the nerve to stand upon the tongue of his wagon in making the ford. The order went out from Moore with curses that any man who violated the rule would be sorry for it; all hands must plunge in and guide their teams across, and we did.

Moore was silent and greatly troubled, for he had heard that he was suspected of having a guilty hand in the killing of Porter. I believe this was the reason why the government sent out from Sidney a detail of cavalry to escort us, as I remember, to the upper reaches of the Snake or Niobrara, when they returned.

Moore began to be abusive to a number of the men, finding fault with them on trumped-up charges, and when we reached Red Cloud, six combinations — that is, twelve wagons — were unloaded of their freight that was intended for the Red Cloud Agency, while the rest went on to Spotted Tail, forty miles north. These wagons were parked and left, and the bulls put into a cavallard and driven along with the train. Six of us were discharged, being paid only for the actual time spent in making the trip to White River; also we were told that we had nothing more coming.

In our little party of bullwhackers, who were marooned in the midst of the Indian country at a time when the Sioux were away from the agency a great deal and were ugly, was a young man named Chapman. I remember just how he looked and what he wore and the songs he sang. He wore an unusually wide-brimmed sombrero, to which was attached a black leather throat latch which was always under his chin. He was a nervy youngster. As the train moved off toward Spotted Tail, Moore remained behind a few minutes to close up some business with the Indian agent; and when he started away on his horse, Chapman followed over a knoll, pulled his gun, and pointed it at Moore's head, demanding the rest of the money he claimed to be coming to him, saying that he was entitled to pay for the time it would take him to get back to Sidney. Moore did not parley, Chapman reported to the rest of us, but handed him ten dollars, — all he had, he said, but not enough.

We were in a bad boat, but not very sorely dismayed, and decided to go up or down the river, I do not remember which way, to Camp Robinson and report the situation. At the stockade entrance, however, we were warned away by a guard, who told us that if we did not clear out in a hurry, we would be given accommodations in the guardhouse. So we started back to the agency buildings on the hill, perhaps a mile or less, and on the way we passed a number of tepees. I looked into one and saw a white man sitting on a buffalo robe reading a book, and was greatly surprised. This man told me his name was Chambers or Chamberlain, I have forgotten which, and that he had been a member of the Chicago Board of Trade and was living with the Indians, — but why, he did not say, or if he did, I have forgotten the reason he gave.

When we reached the agency, we saw several bull teams coming over a distant hill from the north, and knew the outfit was returning empty either to take the Cheyenne or Sidney Trail back to civilization. It was a welcome sight, for by this time we had been surrounded by a number of young bucks, who had begun to pull at our coats and point their arrows at us, and we didn't know what to expect.

The outfit proved to be that owned and operated by two brothers named Smalley. They were in a hurry to get to the south, for bad weather was coming on and no time was to be lost. In fact, they did not even stop at Red Cloud but took the Sidney Trail, their empty wagons being hooked together, eight or ten to a team, while there was a comfortably large cavallard.

I approached one of the Smalleys and told him our troubles, and the two men finally agreed to allow us to accompany them to Sidney, provided we should work as if we were being paid regular wages. This we readily agreed to. One of the Smalleys was driving the loose cattle, and I immediately spelled him while he rode another horse beside his brother. The rest of the fellows relieved some of the bullwhackers; we all took a hand at the cook tricks, and things went along smoothly until we reached a camp known as Willow Springs, fourteen miles north of the Platte River.

An hour or two before we reached this camp it began to snow heavily, and by the time we were unyoked the ground was covered to a depth of two or three inches, and before long there was half a foot on the level. One of my pals took the bulls to a wind-swept spot and started to graze them, and I was assigned to the mess and began the bread making and put on a big pot of beans.

In the Smalley outfit was a white man who seemed to be a privileged character. He was a mystery to all of us until we had been at the Willow Springs camp a few hours, when suddenly, like an apparition, a big buck Indian, with blanket folded about an up-to-date Winchester, stood beside me. He had marched calmly down a near-by knoll and got beside the fire before I knew it. One of the Smalleys appeared on the scene accompanied by the stranger, and the latter immediately began an excited conversation with the buck, to which I listened intently although I could understand but few words one of which was "bacon" and another "bull." It seems that the Indian was demanding a side of bacon and a bull, and that somewhere near at hand was a band of his followers. It also developed, finally, that the stranger, who had been known as a "squaw man," was escaping the vengeance of some of his "Indian relatives," and that they were just over the hill.

The Smalley store of bacon was low, but it was finally decided to give the old buck a large piece, but not a whole side, and that no bulls would be turned over to him. The Indian took the bacon, and as he was about to depart, two more bucks came down the hill slowly, afoot, as the first one had come. They haggled for a while with the stranger and went away as slowly as they came.

But in a few minutes about a dozen young bucks, all with their faces painted in a lurid fashion, came into camp, and the leader, who spoke quite a little English, told the Smalley brothers that we had just one hour to yoke up and start to the Platte and cross it; a refusal meant a fight. So the herd was driven in, and in a blinding snowstorm we started for the river. The snow was soft and light, however, and we made good time. When we reached the river we never stopped, but plunged right into the mush ice and were soon on the sand island.

When the last team crossed over, we could see through the heavy falling snow the band of Indians riding back and forth in the deserted dog town where the Pratt and Farris outfit had camped, and where the tragedy occurred a few weeks before. Before we could get straightened out and make our plans for fording the south branch of the river, a few arrows and a shot or two came among us. All hands stood on wagon tongues and gave the attackers a couple of volleys. It wasn't a bit exciting, and none of us felt for a second that we were in any danger whatever. In truth, not a man in our party even dodged behind a wagon. However, during the little brush, I never caught sight of the squaw man, and believe he plunged his horse into the south channel at the first sign of trouble and headed for Sidney. I never had the pleasure of seeing him again, although it took us only a few days to reach Sidney.

A couple of weeks after we had arrived at the railroad, Chapman came to me and said he was going to collect the rest of the money due him from Pratt and Farris.

He asked me to go with him, and I consented. Walking into the office, Chapman pulled his revolver and said:

"My name is Chapman; you owe me twenty-five dollars and I am here to collect it."

I was amazed to see Charley Moore sitting beside Mr. Pratt, and to hear him say, "Put up your gun and sit down." But this was enough for me, and I left the office and waited outside until Chapman came out and showed me the money. Then I gave him my·gun, went in and, walking straight up to Moore, said:

"I want to talk over the matter of wages I believe due me, but I am not armed."

"How much do you think you have coming?" asked Moore. I told him thirty-five dollars, and he handed it to me as calmly as though he were making change, asked me what I was doing, and what I had heard that was new. I told him the talk had died down about his being implicated in the death of Porter, and he smiled, saying, "Yes, that was a miserable lie; and I'll tell you right now that I believed you and several others who were left at Red Cloud had a hand in starting that story, but I have found out that I was wrong."

That was the last I ever heard of Charley Moore, and I hope that if he is alive, he is prospering. In 1907 I met Mr. Pratt in the City Hall at Omaha at a reception given to myself and one other by Mayor Dahlman. I have recently learned that Mr. Pratt died at a very advanced age. I am sorry that I did not have the time or opportunity to go over with him the stirring incidents of those old wild days, although I did astonish him by saying that I had once whacked bulls for him.

"Mr. Antelope leaped daintily over the tips of the poles and entered the corral."

CHAPTER TWENTY–TWO

RANCHING IN THE LOWER BLACK HILLS

AFTER my experience on the Sidney Trail, there was another season at the Nash ranch in the foothills of the Rocky Mountains. There I assisted the five Nash boys, whose work was mostly play. This consisted of riding the range, going into the hills for poles, and fishing in Dale Creek for native trout; for this was before scientific propagation and before the sportsmen in any considerable number began to whip the mountain streams of that country.

And what wonderful trout we did catch! — and eat in the open, at a campfire, sometimes together with a strip of bacon and homemade bread furnished by the always generous and enthusiastic Mrs. Nash, who had been a friend of my mother's when both were brides in Fond du Lac in its frontier days.

Well do I remember how this good woman cried when I came to the ranch door, after several winters and summers of bullwhacking and all-round adventuring in the northern part of the territory. It was a chilly day, and my garments consisted of a pair of army trousers, badly worn and patched, a pair of heavy cowhide boots, an infantryman's shirt, and a belt of cartridges, a revolver, and a hat — no stockings, no underclothes, no coat, no vest — a fair-weather rig for a bullwhacker. I was amazed to see her cry, and couldn't understand, because I had not been regenerated. I was still wild and woolly, and, as they used to say to make it rhyme, hard to curry. But, as I now remember, she said, shouting to her husband:

"Albert, Albert, come here quick; here's Will Hooker!" and then, speaking to me, added: "Oh, I am glad your mother can't see you! You must have a coat; and you go right down in the creek and strip everything off, and I'll get you some of the boys' clothes."

I couldn't understand what she meant, for I was really comfortable and felt natural. But the good woman persisted and handed me a bar of soap and a towel; and I went to the creek, an ice-cold, fast-running mountain stream, where I left everything except my boots, which were new, and put on the clothes brought to me by Ben Nash.

I had neither money nor valuables of any kind, and while my stomach was empty, I remember that I was perfectly happy and not at all worried about the future. However, I had some plans, one of which was to make only a short stay at the ranch and as soon as possible get to a bull outfit somewhere — I didn't know where. However, Mr. and Mrs. Nash had other opinions, and they were strong. I was to stay at the ranch for a few weeks or months, and then try to get a job on the Union Pacific Railroad.

The Nash ranch was in those beautiful Lower Black Hills near Sherman Station, the highest point on the Union Pacific. His buildings stood on the site of Dale City — a shack town located ahead of the railroad in anticipation of its arrival in the little Dale Valley; but the builders did not select that route.

Mr. Nash's brand was "Circle N," and his range extended over the Harney Flats and a portion of the Laramie Plains beyond. He had a large herd of cattle and many horses. The cattle, with the exception of the usual so-called "cats and dogs," — the corral herd, — were rarely seen except at the annual round-ups; but it was customary to keep close track of the cows, bulls, horses, and a few pet sheep owned by the boys. It was my duty to go out to the Flats at least once a week, usually with one of the five Nash boys, round up the "cats and dogs," and fetch them to the corral, where they would be kept a few days and then turned loose.

On one occasion I undertook the job alone, and I spent a whole day at it from sunup to sundown. I found most of the cattle and horses feeding together, but counting them, I discovered a number missing; so I mounted the highest piece of land near by and surveyed the country for miles around, locating several cows and a couple of young bulls, which I started toward the larger herd. As I mounted a hill a half mile away, I saw clearly that an antelope was feeding with the cattle, being quite surrounded by them.

Now, to those of my readers who do not know it, let me say that even at that period, when there were tens of thousands of antelope on the plains, that animal was about as shy as a fox is today in the state of New York, and it was very difficult to get in range of him; therefore what happened is the more remarkable.

I resolved to undertake what I believed to be the utterly impossible — drive that antelope, with the herd, to the corral and capture him alive. Therefore I slowly but surely rounded up all the stock, keeping it around the antelope as well as I could, made no sound whatever, and gradually worked the herd along until I came to a round-top hill in sight of the ranch buildings and the corral.

Standing near the back door of the Nash home was Benny Nash — then, he says, of the tender age of six years. He saw me wave my hand and motion for him to let down the poles of the corral gate. As he also saw the antelope at the same time, and understood the sign of silence I gave by putting my hand over my mouth, he moved quickly, letting down the poles and finding a hiding place for himself behind the spring-house at the creek, until he saw Mr. Antelope leap daintily over the tips of the poles and enter the corral, when he came out from his hiding place and helped me make the imprisonment secure.

We had a full-grown antelope, one that could not possibly be tamed. So within a few hours his carcass was hung by the hind legs in a temporary abattoir; and we had venison, although there was nothing novel about that.

Ben Nash is now a retired railroad engineer living in Cheyenne; and he says he has told this story a great many times, and believes I am the only man who ever rounded up and corralled a live, full-grown antelope. That is probably not so. It is undoubtedly true that both Indians and white men rigged up traps and drove whole herds of antelope into them; in fact, I am sure they did.

In the Lower Black Hills, at the edges of the Laramie Plains, there were many little broad valleys that narrowed as they reached the high land, affording the best kind of trap at points where fences could be built and openings left that could be easily and quickly closed after a herd had entered. However, Mr. Nash says many old-timers to whom he has related these facts have shown signs of being incredulous; and these lines are being published without any thought or belief that I may have done something that no one else ever did, but partly to fortify the story for Mr. Nash, who may now point to this book for additional authority.

"Lon put his nose into the door and stood there."

CHAPTER TWENTY–THREE

LON — OF THE BROWN FAMILY

THE experiences I had with the wild-animal life out in that famous game country during my bullwhacking and ranch days would fill a book. The country was then alive, not only with antelope and deer and elk, but with such predatory animals as coyotes, wolves, and mountain lions. Bears were also abundant.

Perhaps the most remarkable of my experiences came in connection with old Lon — a member of the Brown Family. At least, Lon was one of the cleverest of the animals whose acquaintance I made.

We called him Lon, because Alonzo Hendricks met him first and knew him better than any of the rest of us on Cactus Creek.

Lon was a member of the Brown Family — the brown-bear family — sometimes called cinnamon; and if he wasn't a humorist and hadn't the clever nature of his neighbor, the fox, then I am no good judge of humor or cleverness. And Lon was no coward, either, although he had acquired a habit of being absent nearly every time I happened to cross his path armed. If I walked fifteen rods from the door of my cabin without a rifle, I'd meet Lon, and he would stand up on his haunches, stick out his long tongue, and laugh. Yes, he laughed — not a real guffaw, but his beady old eyes would twinkle, and he'd twist his mouth into the most comical grin, and hold whatever spot he happened to squat down on. But when I was armed, I couldn't get near him, although I might be positive that he was around, for Lon was not clever enough to cover up his tracks either winter or summer; but he knew how to make himself scarce.

One day I set a trap for Lon without intending to do it. I had accumulated a lot of empty tin cans, stone jars, and jelly glasses in a lean-to of my cabin, and as I wanted to store a couple of bales of skins in the lean-to, I put the accumulation of cans and jars in a gunny sack and threw them in a heap just at the edge of a small grove ten rods from my cabin door.

There had been corn, peas, tomatoes, raspberry and strawberry jam, and other delicacies in some of the jars and cans. I think there was some honey in one glass jar that had a big open top. It was a fine fall day when I cleaned house, and the flies were still numerous, for there had been no frost or freezing nights, and the sweets attracted the flies. I noticed this as I happened to pass that way, and I also noted — I had my gun along — that Lon had been there; in fact, I believed I could hear him faintly. Anyway, I scented him. So I took a wide circle; first, however, I walked away in a straight line in a direction just opposite to where I believed Lon to be hiding and possibly watching me. I hurried as if I had picked up a trail or had important business to transact a long way from there. But I crept back to another point where I could get a full view of the cabin and the collection of old tins, and I sat there from noon until sundown without discovering the movement of a blade of grass, to say nothing of a bush, on any side of my unconscious trap.

So I went into the cabin, fried my bacon, and in twenty minutes was eating it, when I thought just for fun I'd get up, go out the back way, — I couldn't see the "trap" from my window, — and take another look before dark. I stepped clear out of the cabin, without a gun, and, if you please, there stood Lon backed up against a sapling with a honey jar tightly fastened on his nose, with both front paws clawing desperately at it. He saw me as plainly as you can see the house across the street when there is no obstruction, and he only stopped clawing long enough to give me a careless once-over to see if I had a gun. Seeing that I was unarmed, he resumed his efforts to get the jar off his nose. I pretended not to see him, and slowly entered the cabin, grabbed my Winchester, and jumped out into the open quicker than scat. But, do you know, that old cuss had disappeared as if the earth had opened and swallowed him up.

Another time I nearly got Lon, when I found him in trouble and almost too busy to do guard duty and eat blackberries at the same time. It was in August, and I never saw so many berries. Lon's home was on a mountain several miles from my cabin, at a point above timber line. His den was at the end of a long, winding path, and in a mass of broken rocks that would defy most men to negotiate. It was a regular hell's half-acre, and I trailed Lon to the spot more than a dozen times, only to find him safely hidden when I arrived and unwilling to come out even when I kept a vigil of twelve hours. I even went there without a rifle, boldly but not recklessly, for I could outrun the old boy — I was sure of that.

But there was nothing to eat where Lon lived, and he was obliged to come down to the timber; and pretty far down, too, if he was looking for dessert, the berries growing at a point more than three and a half miles from timber line.

It was on one of his berry forays that I nearly got him. He must have been very hungry, for he was in the bushes threshing around like mad, striking right and left, and rubbing his eyes in a most human manner when I came upon him. I soon discovered that he was in a perfect cloud of mosquitoes, and they had attacked him in such numbers that he was nearly blinded. At that he scented me and made a dash into a thicket, and I let go at random four or five shots. And they were the only shots I ever fired at Lon.

Many times after that he came down for blackberries, but it was in the night, and while I knew he was there and could hear him snort and slap at the mosquitoes, I couldn't locate him well enough to get a fairly decent shot at him. I didn't try to spoil his feast, which I figured was sufficiently beset with difficulties; and I thought he was entitled to quarter if willing to battle with millions of mosquitoes for something to top off his meal of roots, mice, and cones that he had labored hard, perhaps all day, to get.

Lon was almost friendly one time, and I thought he was going to make a social call in my cabin kitchen. I was frying ham, and he put his nose into the door and stood there as much as to say, "If you'll promise not to shoot, I'll come in — be decent now, and neighborly." But I had my eye on his fine robe, and, wanting it, reached for my gun and he was gone. Nothing is so attractive to a bear as the smell of fried ham.

Since then I have regretted that I didn't share my dinner with Lon, for he really was a mighty decent neighbor, and I wasn't.

"I helped on the drive."

CHAPTER TWENTY–FOUR

A TURN AT COWBOY LIFE

THE plans of my good foster-mother, Mrs. Nash, to get me away from the rough life of bullwhacking succeeded only in part. I did not go back to the railroad, as she had suggested; neither did I return to the old freight trail. Instead, after a few weeks, I went to Laramie City, where a Mr. Andrews, an insurance man, on the recommendation of Mr. Nash, attempted to utilize my services in his office as a clerk; but I never succeeded in doing anything well for him except sweep out the office, and the tenure of that job terminated abruptly when he discovered that I knew nothing at all about figures.

Over the mountains I back-trailed to Cheyenne in the caboose of Sam Smith, freight conductor, and in a few days I found myself in a lonely spot known as Chalk Bluffs — being the only resident there. I feel justified in claiming to be the first settler of that now well-settled district in agricultural northern Colorado.

A man in Cheyenne had discovered that the soil in that rattlesnake-ridden wild place was tillable ground where irrigation was not necessary to raise a crop of potatoes, and he had planted a couple of acres that were just beginning to grow. He built a miserable dugout, dumped off a side of bacon, a sack of flour, and a few other things, and left me there with a hoe.

He instructed me particularly to keep a sharp lookout for cattle, although there were no ranches anywhere in the vicinity. No human beings were near; but there were thousands of swallows in the bluffs and hundreds of rattlesnakes, while on the uplands were antelope in herds and packs of wolves. The so-called Texas Trail, however, ran three miles east of the Chalk Bluffs potato patch, and my new boss suspected that at almost any time the Texans would find the grass in the little valley richer and in larger quantities and would drive their herds to the westward. He was justified in this belief, for within ten days of my arrival, as I lolled one warm afternoon in front of the dugout, I heard the far-off voice of a herder and the rumbling sound of what seemed to be a train of cars or a storm. It soon grew louder and louder, an indescribable noise that took me to the ground near the dugout above the creek bottom. As I reached the top, there came plunging toward me a magnificently mounted horseman, who shouted:

"Hello, son, what the dickens ye doin' here? By George, you're lucky we headed 'em 'tother way, 'cause they would a-been on top o' yer roof!"

I had killed a half-dozen big rattlers that day, and my reply was something like this:

"I'm watchin' some 'taters tryin' to grow down in yon bottoms, but spendin' most of my time killin' rattlers," and I took off my sombrero and showed him a triple band of rattles I had plucked off during my ten days' killings.

"How much ye gettin' for this job?" asked the herder.

"Thirty dollars a month," I replied, "and found," meaning grub. "But," I added, "I'd like to get out o' here — do you need any more help?"

"We sure do," he replied quickly. "Can you ride?"

Within the next few minutes I was astride a fine herd-horse; for several other men had arrived, the cattle had calmed down, and they were working the herd along the banks of the creek that straggled at the great desert and at the bluffs. I had been homesick for the first time in my life, and had not the Texans happened along just as they did, I should have hoofed it to Cheyenne within a week.

I helped on the drive to a point just east of Fort Laramie, where the herd was delivered to a company that had selected a range near what is now Torrington.

Through my disobedience, while on the night trick from twelve to two with the foreman of the outfit, I stampeded the herd of several thousand head of cattle. It was a pitch-black night, not a star in sight; and because Indians were on the warpath, a detail of United States Cavalry was with us after we crossed the Union Pacific, which convinces me that the owners of the stock must have had a strong pull with the government, or that the cattle were to be fed to fill a government Indian contract.

When I rode out from camp to the herd with the boss, he warned me repeatedly not to get out of my saddle until he returned, and instructed me, in case of a stampede, to follow the herd and keep up the laggards — nothing else. He would lead and gradually turn the cattle back to the bedding ground. Every animal was lying down, all quiet and serene so far as I could see; so I dismounted, drove my iron picket into the sod, and prepared to stretch out on the ground.

Then what do you think happened that made every critter in that herd leap to its feet? In throwing on my saddle, I had doubled under in some way either the leather flap or the pad, or had twisted one of my cinches. As I dismounted, the horse took this first opportunity to make himself comfortable by vigorously shaking himself. The herd was up in an instant; but my horse knew his business if I didn't — and I certainly didn't, for this was my first and last experience in a stampede. The first thing I realized was that my horse was making some frightful jumps, and that the picket-pin at the end of my long rawhide lariat was now and then hitting me in the back. I soon drew it in and obeyed my instructions to keep up the laggards, and I did it for miles — I do not know how many.

The whole camp turned out and the boss turned on me, after it was all over and broad daylight and a heavy rain falling, with: "Young feller, you got off that hoss!"

I dodged the issue, for lying in several washouts were dead and wounded cattle, how many I do not remember. I felt justified in making a strenuous denial. What helped me more than anything else was the fact that at almost the same instant that I dismounted, there was just the faintest flash of lightning, which I did not see, but which the foreman saw. But he said that at the same moment he had heard a strange noise from my direction.

The next day as we renewed the slow process of grazing the herd along toward its destination, one of the herders rode up beside me and said that the soldier who was on guard at the camp when the stampede started told him he distinctly heard a horse shake its saddle, and he (the herder) wanted to get it straight from me whether I dismounted or whether it was the foreman. He himself believed it was the foreman. I refused to own up, fearing that he was pumping me for the boss.

A few nights later, when I rode into camp from my two-hour watch with the herd, I rode fast and was almost on the soldier guard — the same one — before the sleepy fellow discovered me. He sang out quickly: "Who comes there?"

I did not answer until he pressed his Springfield against my side and added, "Friend or foe?"

"Friend," I mumbled; but he never had a chance to say "Advance, friend, and give the countersign," for in two more jumps I was off my horse and with temper ruffled started back to the guard with a revolver leveled ready to make him apologize. However, I didn't get very far because a sergeant knocked the weapon from my hands, for which act I am more than thankful. Then the guard began to upbraid me for getting off my horse and stampeding the herd. There was so much noise between us that the foreman crawled out of his blankets and took a hand, saying:

"It's none o' your business if he did, but he didn't. The first cow that riz up riz exactly in front of me the very minit there was a flash o' lightnin'. I heard that noise, too, but it must 'a-been somethin' else, maybe one of the hosses in camp."

It is rather late in life to make this confession, but if that foreman is alive and reads this, I wish he would write to me and give me his name, for I owe him a word of appreciation for helping me out of a tight pinch.

"I trudged on alone day after day."

CHAPTER TWENTY–FIVE

A TOUCH OF TRAMP LIFE

WHEN I was paid off, I walked to Fort Laramie, and then down to the Chugwater, where I joined a returning bull outfit to Cheyenne. This outfit went into camp on Crow creek, south of Cheyenne, and I stayed in Cheyenne hoping to get another job at bullwhacking; but there was no freight to haul and consequently nothing to do, and I was almost penniless, but happy and care free as usual.

Thousands of men were then treking into the Black Hills. I decided to go with them into Custer City, but failed to make a connection. At about this time I struck up an acquaintance with a Welsh miner who had come on from the lead mines of Joplin, Missouri. He had gone part way to Custer and turned back when he met dozens of others returning with discouraging reports. He was going back to Missouri, and "hoof it all the way," he said. "Why not go with me?" he asked.

I readily consented, for to me at that time of life it seemed to matter little which way I turned. There was promise of adventure, at least, and perhaps fortune at the lead mines. So we started to hike from Cheyenne, Wyoming Territory, to Omaha, Nebraska — five hundred and seventeen miles.

By the time we reached North Platte we had, I think, less than a dollar between us. Most of the time there was no place to spend even that, for it must be remembered that there were few settlements at that time west of Grand Island. We managed to exist, however, because section men were kind-hearted and gave us food. Tramps were few and far between, and most of these good men were glad to get reports about the gold stampede to the Hills.

Finally, shortly after leaving North Platte, my Missouri partner quit me to swing a pick and shovel on a section gang that was short-handed. I was mad as a hatter, but trudged on alone day after day along the dreary wastes of sand, occasionally stopping for a few hours at some section house, where the men were uniformly kind.

Somewhere in the vicinity of Grand Island, where the land was more fertile (or perhaps it was near Kearny — I am not sure), I tried to catch the caboose of a freight train as it pulled out of a long sidetrack, but encountered a brakeman on the rear platform who wore a heavy boot which he planted in my stomach. I grabbed his boot. We both fell upon the track, and he began to strike me in the face. But I was not now the weak boy who went to Wyoming perhaps to die of tuberculosis, so I rolled him off the rails and upon the dump and pommeled him good and hard.

By this time I observed the train had slowed down and the entire crew was coming back; so I loosened my grip on the brakeman's throat and dashed off the right-of-way into heavy sand. The crew came after me, but I knew how to tread sand better than any of them and was soon a long way out of danger.

It was coming night, and I wandered over the sand for an hour or so, finally finding myself in a veritable oasis in which there was a milk house a long way from a sod homestead. I waited until the light went out in the house and then entered the milk house and regaled myself. There were several swinging shelves with a couple of dozen pans of rich milk. I kept no record of the number of pans I emptied, and perhaps I had better not even guess; but I will say that then and there I drank all the milk I needed to last me until this day in 1924 — and that was fifty years ago.

Perhaps I would not have the antipathy for milk that I now have had I not found something else in that milk house — a bottle of port wine. I took this with me when I left before the first streak of day. All of it had disappeared before I reached the platform of a railroad freight house, either at Kearny or Grand Island, where I lay down and went to sleep. Some time later I was wakened by a lively shaking I was receiving from a rough-looking individual. He showed me the biggest "tin star" in the world and announced that he was a constable. I made no attempt to resist, for he was a big fellow. Also I was deathly sick, as he soon realized when he got me standing against the freight house.

I was headed for the calaboose again, and I remembered my Uncle John Peacock. Would this constable turn me loose if I put up a good plea, I wondered? I decided to beg off, and did a successful job, for he agreed that if I would not stop until I came to the second milepost beyond town I should be free.

At Council Bluffs, Iowa, I found a job hauling wood by team from the hills to a brickyard located at the far end of the main street, and I held it until the wood was all delivered. Then I went to Omaha, joined a circus as a roustabout, traveled through Iowa to Illinois, where I turned northward and entered the harvest fields. Finally, after a few years of steady work, I returned with a well-filled pocketbook to old Wisconsin.

I was ready by this time to settle down. My wild experiences had taught me many things of no value and headed me into harmful ways which would have spelled ruin for me if I had not turned a sharp corner — as I am happy to say I did.

Mr. Hooker standing on the site of his dugout on La Bonte Creek,
Wyoming, where he lived during the winter of 1874–1875.

CHAPTER TWENTY-SIX

BACK-TRAILING IN OLD WYOMING

NEARLY fifty years had slipped away. The years, filled
to the full with varied adventures and strenuous duties,
mainly in connection with the newspaper world, where
I rose gradually from typesetting to the "editor's uneasy
chair," gave me little time even for memory excursions
over the old trails. Not that I had forgotten my days
in the wilds of the West — but they, like the old trails,
were being gradually obliterated by the activities of the
throbbing present.

Then came a call from the Historical Department of
the state of Wyoming. My pioneer reminiscences were
needed to help round out the records. It was a pleasant
reminder that I had played a part in the pioneering of a
great state. This thought had hardly occurred to me,
even though my coal-black hair had changed during the
swiftly passing years to snowy white.

Ellis T. Peirce ("Bear Tracks"), early-day sheriff of the Black Hills region, and a terror to horse thieves and "road agents."

I was invited to go out to Wyoming and deliver an address on "Early Days in Wyoming," in the senate chamber of the State Capitol in Cheyenne. And I went — this time in a Pullman car. I went also up to Douglas, Wyoming, and addressed a large gathering at the County Fair held in the fall of 1921. This thriving city, by the way, is situated about twelve miles from the site of the old dugout I built and in which I had wintered with Nick Huber.

On the site of my old dugout I found the very door posts I cut with my own hands in the fall of 1874, and the owner of a ranch near by presented me with a rusted part of a gun, a buckle, and other things I had left when hastily departing in the spring of 1875, because of a report of an Indian raid.

John Hunton drove me to old Fort Fetterman — what is left of it — in an automobile. The Burlington Railroad runs within half a mile of the fort site, but the trains do not stop there. Only one ranch house is where the fort was.

The old wooden building, once a home for the officers, was occupied by a ranchman and his family, a few cows and chickens wandered over what was the parade ground, and, all together, everything seemed desolate. Off to the north, perhaps three or four miles distant, in a vast cup formed by the sloping plains, was in clear view a station on another railroad, a water tank, several houses, a corral or two, and a string of freight cars on a long siding. The cup, too, was checkerboarded with wire fences, and here and there were green squares of alfalfa. What a change!

A mound of adobe and stone ruins, the former melted by rain and baked into fantastic shapes by the suns of many summers and resembling almost anything but the ruins of a building, is the last remnant of the old storehouse where we bullwhackers used to unload bacon, corn, flour, and other supplies. It seemed the only thing worth photographing, and so I snapped a picture and walked away, my mind filled with a mixture of sentiment and wonder at the metamorphosis.

Then I returned to a point on the south line of the old parade ground and paced off as well as I could with the aid of landmarks the location of the guardhouse, where, on several occasions, I slept, ate dry bread, and drank alkali water a week at a time because of simple infractions of military regulations which applied to soldier and civilian alike. I could hear little old Major Kane, red-faced and haughty, order my punishment for venturing on forbidden ground to get a view of the first Gatling gun that was sent west of the muddy Missouri.

But all hate had left my heart on this September day, in the year 1921, when I stood on this spot and upon a tablet of paper scribbled the following:

> In buckskin garb, 'twas here I stood,
> When driving oxen hauling wood;
> The major shouted, "Guard, come here —
> This man is acting mighty queer!"

> With bayonet pointed at my hip
> Began my second guardhouse trip;
> Nor falter did I when he said:
> "Quick! march! Or by —— you're dead!"

Then I wandered over to the spot where Sutler Tillotson used to take one dollar for a tumblerful of whisky
that produced blind staggers in a customer before he
could get outside the entrance.

Not far away are oil fields producing millions of
gallons every year; alfalfa, wheat, corn, and sugar beets
grow on the plains and in the valleys that were in my
day supposed to be part of the "Great American Desert,"
familiar on every map in school geographies in the
sixties.

The old trails are brown on the hillsides, unused, for
they are usually fenced in by wire, while hard-surfaced
auto roads go straight ahead up hill and down vale,
following county lines drawn by surveyors who pioneered
after I left to live in city canyons — lost in the ebb and
flow of the human tide of a great metropolis.

And when I back-trailed in 1921, I wished I could
again undergo all the hardships where the sky is clear,
the air is fresh, and the handclasp is warm.

A week later I was riding into old Fort Laramie, 105
miles east of the site of Fort Fetterman, also on the
North Platte River, in a taxicab! My companion was
the Hon. John Hunton. The last time I entered this
oasis in the then great desert, I drove seven yoke of
oxen attached to two big canvas-covered wagons loaded
with more than four tons of shelled corn, while Mr.
Hunton, owner of the wagon train, rode a splendid
horse, directing the movement. A band was playing,
away out here in the wilds of America, jackasses brayed,
soldiers not on duty swarmed around us, together with a
number of half-breed Canadian-French Indians, all
anxious to hear the news from along the trail we had
traveled for several weeks. It was a picturesque sight,
but not quite appreciated at the time.

But now, in 1921, after Uncle Sam has relinquished his title to the 34,560 acres comprising the Fort Laramie military reservation, what do we find?

It was a pitch-dark night when we left the train at the station about four miles north and entered a taxi which whirled us across a well-built bridge over the North Platte and along a sandy-loamy road cut deep into the earth, with wire fences on either side all the way to the few ruins and

John Hunton, the freighting magnate, as Mr. Hooker knew him in 1874.

one or two well-kept houses at the fort. We passed great fields of alfalfa and corn, and as the clouds moved, the moon disclosed the roofless hospital building and the sashless windows in walls that still contain the iron bars of the original guardhouse.

The sway-backed roof of the sutler's store, built of adobe and plastered without, supporting a tottering chimney, was disclosed. Oaken doors, the planks of which were held together with bands of iron and crude hinges fashioned by some company blacksmith, perhaps as early as 1849 or 1850, were there as firmly as they were when Indians lurked on a dark night like this, waiting for some indiscreet soldier or civilian inhabitant of the post to show his head as a mark for an arrow.

As we rode rapidly up a slight grade, I ventured to remark, "Here were the warehouses," and Mr. Hunton replied that my bump of location had not been impaired by living in a metropolis these many years. Then, as we advanced, we came to a board gate, not far from the old parade ground, and opening it we entered a corral-like space, in which a number of milch cows were lying, chewing their cuds.

"Here is a stable," I ventured.

"Yes," replied Mr. Hunton, "this *is* now a stable; but General Charles King immortalized it in one of his novels as 'Bedlam,' a social gathering place for army officers where there were frequent high jinks with sparkling champagne that was hauled across the wilderness by ox teams. Yes, it is a stable used by one of the owners of this property; and here in this stone building are his chickens, as fine a lot as you ever saw, too; and they are roosting where the powder was stored when you last came here, for this is the old magazine."

Mr. Hunton lived in a very substantial building. He gave me a comfortable bed in a room once used by natty army officers who came to the frontier from West Point to fight with Red Cloud and his warriors.

In the old sutler's store we rummaged among the débris that has accumulated in a span of more than two average lifetimes. On a top shelf, covered with fully half an inch of dust, we found two boxes of cartridges. They had been placed there, Mr. Hunton believed, by some former clerk — perhaps himself — more than fifty years ago, for this make of cartridge has not been used since the early sixties, and it was invented in the fifties and used by the army and others for a very short time, being replaced by the Sharps, also paper-covered. We found also an account book of great interest to us. It lay in a pile of other documents of a day long past — before the telephone, electric lights, and automobiles — in the day of the ox team and the express rider, the

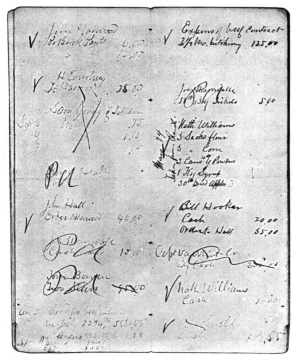

A page from an account book kept by John Hunton in 1874–1875. The Sam Young entered here (third name in left-hand column), also called Harry Young, later became a traveling passenger agent for the Oregon Railroad Navigation Company; in after years he wrote the book, "Hard Knocks." Nath Williams (right-hand column) was the wagon boss who started Mr. Hooker out as a bullwhacker. The author remembers well the dried apples mentioned in the item above his name; and that was fifty years ago.

scout, and the stagecoach — and in it were notations made by Mr. Hunton on September 14, 1867, fifty-four years ago to the day. I tore out the leaves to add to the Historical Museum at Cheyenne.

Fort Laramie! Romantic spot in American history, given over to cattle and chickens — a fast-disappearing mass of crumbling walls with but one resident who saw it in all its glory — when it was an oasis in a vast unoccupied territory, a welcome resting place and refuge for hunter, trapper, trader, bullwhacker, and immigrant who came either on business or for protection from hostile tribes of Indians. That man is John Hunton, who, in 1890, was the last of a long list of post traders at the fort when the government issued the order for its abandonment, due to the fact that the Indian question had become obsolete.

THE TAMING OF PIPESTONE[1]

Pipestone sat on his horse,
Holding a twisted hair halter in his left hand;
His right shaded his eyes as he faced the burning sun,
Whose rays polished his copper skin
From shoulder to toes;
For there was naught in the way of raiment
On his body but a breechclout.

The smoke of a distant campfire,
Where freighters had stopped
For a noonday bite, had paused Pipestone
And his loping cayuse. . . .
The hickory bow,
The nest of flinted arrows,
Were fondled.

Deep in a coulee Pipestone tethered Pinto;
For Pinto stood too high above the sage. . . .
Crawling . . .
Crawling . . .
Snake-like, up, up, over the intervening hills,
Pipestone reached the camp's edge . . .
Behind a rock.

Ten . . . twenty . . . thirty white men, he counted.
Crawling . . .
Crawling . . .
To Pinto . . . sleepy Pinto in the coulee.
"*Istinma? . . . San-pa-ya!*" [2]
And Pinto's every hair stood on end
As he sped on with Pipestone. . . .

[1] Written by the author several years ago for the *Erie Railroad Magazine*.
[2] Sleep? Now go!

Bare legs squeezed Pinto's ribs. . . .
The hickory bow beat into the tender of his groin. . . .
An arrow point pressed into his back
When his unshod feet stumbled. . . .
Pipestone was in a hurry
To reach the tepee hunting camp
Of Glass Arrow, his brother. . . .

Lodgepoles, dragged over the ashen sage
And across the grass
By other Pintos, half starved,
Brought the buffalo hunters of Red Cloud
To the banks of Chugwater Creek
Before the next sunrise. . . .
Oxen grazed near the corral of wagons.

But all was silent . . .
Save the rustle of the light wind
That came with the first streak of day. . . .
On their bellies Pipestone . . . Glass Arrow . . . others
Crawled . . .
Crawled. . . .
Then a blanket under a prairie schooner moved.

Pipestone . . . Glass Arrow . . . others . . . hugged the
    ground
As if they loved it. . . .
A white man sat upright . . .
And an arrow, curved from the sagebrush,
Made a rent in the blanket.
Swish! . . . Two more. . . . Swish! . . . Swish! . . .
. . . Crack! Bang! Bang! . . . Flash! . . . Bang!
Bang! — crack, crack, bang!

Sunup. . . . The long wagon train strung out over the
    mesa.
Another day's drive began. . . .

At noon, the incident forgotten — almost. . . .
Only one man limped . . . from an arrow.

Pipestone . . . Glass Arrow . . .
Talked it over . . . and decided . . .
No more hunt um white man; hunt um buffalo.

Crawling . . .
Crawling . . .
They stalked the buffalo,
For the buffalo was defenseless. . . . They stalked the
    buffalo
Because —
The white man on that daybreak occasion
Introduced into Indian warfare
The repeating rifle.